Happy Habits
for
Every Couple

Happy Habits
for
Every Couple

ROGER and **KATHI LIPP**

HARVEST HOUSE PUBLISHERS
EUGENE, OREGON

Cover by Franke Design and Illustration, Excelsior, Minnesota

Cover photos © themacx, -M-I-S-H-A-/ iStock

Published in association with the literary agency of WordServe Literary Group, Ltd., www.wordserveliterary.com.

HAPPY HABITS FOR EVERY COUPLE

Copyright © 2009 Kathi Lipp
Published by Harvest House Publishers
Eugene, Oregon 97402
www.harvesthousepublishers.com

Library of Congress Cataloging-in-Publication Data
  Lipp, Kathi, 1967-
  [Marriage project]
  Happy habits for every couple / Kathi Lipp and Roger Lipp.
      pages cm
  Rev. ed. of: The marriage project. c2009.
  ISBN 978-0-7369-5573-7 (pbk.)
  ISBN 978-0-7369-5574-4 (eBook)
  1. Marriage—Religious aspects—Christianity—Textbooks. I. Title.
BV835.L53 2014
248.8'44—dc23
                                                                        2014022632

Printed in the United States of America

14 15 16 17 18 19 20 21 22 / VP-JH / 10 9 8 7 6 5 4 3 2 1

This book is lovingly dedicated to my parents,
Bill and Connie Richerson.

Thanks for the care, love, and support shown to me and to
everyone that God has brought into my life. Every child should be
blessed to have parents that encourage with such reckless abandon.

I pray that through your legacy of love,
I will have the same fearlessness and boldness when it comes
to encouraging my own kids to pursue their dreams.

Contents

Laying a Foundation: Preparing for *Happy Habits for Every Couple*

Building Up Your Marriage: Launching *Happy Habits for Every Couple*

Week One Projects

Introduction
Roger Lipp

To the Men

Come on guys, admit it. If you're like me, you've started a lot of projects before. Some of them lie in various stages of "done" or "done-enough."

For me, reading an entire book is a monumental challenge. I recently went through my bookshelves and found all kinds of great books that I've purchased. Man, do I need to read that one. Wouldn't it be great if I mastered that bit of knowledge. My books call out to me.

But as I was pulling the books down in one last admission that I probably won't read them, I noticed a strange pattern. Most of my books have something odd about them: they all have a bookmark in them somewhere between chapters 2 and 3. Alas, I started the challenge, but then faded out. Each book I pick up, I start off with great intentions of completing the book and learning or putting into practice the great advice or ideas found within its pages. But something happens between chapter 1 and chapter 3. Some other project comes along, some other item of great importance develops ("hey, I've been meaning to fix the garage door"), and my best intentions get set aside leaving a memorial marker.

So let me make a few bold promises. First, this is an easy read, even for those of us who may not be into reading that much. Second, you'll discover that *Happy Habits for Every Couple* is a lot of fun. Who knows, you might find some fun in some unexpected ways. Finally, this book is worth seeing it through. We all admit that our relationship with our wife is the most important relationship we have, but it's all too easy to let it ride (a strategy that is suspect in Vegas and downright devastating in relationships). See this through. You will be amazed at the change in yourself and your spouse!

To the Women

Wives, you may have noticed, but there are a lot of different kinds of men. Some are eager to work on relationships. Others would be happy to swim alligator-infested waters for you, but don't ask them how they feel about their relationship with you. But whatever kind of guy you're hooked up with, grace is needed as you approach *Happy Habits for Every Couple*.

Since we encourage everyone to do this with at least one other couple, there might be a temptation to do some unhealthy comparisons. ("Wow, your husband filled your room with flowers? Mine only bought me a card!") Every guy is different. Every relationship is in a different place. Every circumstance is different. Enjoy the process and don't compare us (you may have noticed that we have pretty fragile egos). Give us credit for just being willing to do this very outside-our-comfort-zone kind of project.

We need all the positive reinforcement we can get.

A Word from Kathi on the Writing of This Book

You know how in your marriage some tasks naturally fall to you and some naturally fall to your spouse? Roger makes the bed and I make sure that everyone has at least one pair of presentable underwear in their drawers. Roger pays the bills and I make sure that we all are fed each night.

But not all of our roles fall along traditional gender lines. Somehow, making sure the garbage gets to the curb has fallen to me. But I can't really complain because on our morning and evening walks, Roger is the designated pooper scooper. (Jake, the puggle, thanks you. And so do our neighbors.)

So when it came to this book, we both went with our strengths. I'm the writer of the family, and trying to go back and forth in two voices seemed confusing, so I put the words to the page.

But let's be clear—every project, every idea has been thought up, executed, and test-driven by both Roger and me and about 200 friends at Church on the Hill in San Jose, California. Roger is the more creative of us two, and the more romantic most of the time, so his fingerprints are all over these pages.

We wanted a practical guide that brought you both out of your comfortable marriage box just a little bit. Between the two of us, and all the contributing husbands and wives, I think we have just the thing for you here.

Here's to enjoying your marriage a little more today than yesterday.

A Leader's Perspective

When I first heard about *Happy Habits for Every Couple* I was sitting in a seminar for Christian communicators. The person presenting asked the audience to shout out topics that churches should address in their sermons, and Kathi Lipp stood up one row in front of me and shared her heart for *Happy Habits for Every Couple*. I wanted to stand up and say, "You're from the church I pastor. Why haven't I heard about this yet?" At the end of the seminar I nearly tackled Kathi in the lobby to talk details about piloting her idea in our church. For me, *Happy Habits for Every Couple* was much more than a book. I sensed this would be a movement of God.

As the lead pastor of Church on the Hill, I invited our entire church to put their marriages on project status for 21 days (plus some prep time for couples). During those four weeks the Sunday messages were focused on understanding men's and women's unique qualities (and quirkiness) in order for us to become people who were building health into our marriages. We provided small groups for couples to share their daily victories and woes.

Happy Habits for Every Couple is about improving your marriage relationship. For 21 days you will focus your time, energy, and finances on developing happy habits for your marriage, which means you'll need to put other areas of your life on the back burner.

I get the fact that some of you are thinking, "But my marriage isn't broken!" By jumping into *Happy Habits for Every Couple* you aren't admitting failure or crisis; you may just want to improve the good marriage you already have. And most of us have an innate sense that our marriages have room for improvement or you wouldn't be holding this book right now. Whether your marriage is in crisis or your marriage feels healthy, these 21 days will help you build a marriage that does more than survive—it thrives!

So far this might sound intimidating because you've read other marriage books that had you focus on all your weaknesses and failures. Not this book. Each daily project is about encouraging your spouse rather than listing your five most irritating habits that drive your spouse insane. The essence of *Happy Habits for Every Couple* is about becoming a person of encouragement who serves the one you love. There is tremendous power in these pages that you're about to discover as you practice the art of encouragement.

As a pastor I want our church couples to have the best marriages in our community. However, as I write these words, another story just came across my desk of a couple in our church who felt unfulfilled and found themselves in the throes of an affair. This is a couple that hasn't worked through *Happy Habits for Every Couple*...at least not yet.

God, the author of marriage, designed your marriage to be the most intimate relationship of your life. Your marriage was intended to be filled with joy, laughter, authenticity, transparency, hope, encouragement, and great sex! Why then are so many marriages simply trying to survive instead of thrive?

It's easy for us to forget that people flourish with encouragement. Every marriage should be a refuge of encouragement, and I pray you discover what I did, that as you engage in *Happy Habits for Every Couple,* God will reignite His original design for your marriage, and you'll rediscover how great your spouse really is.

Make no mistake about it: your time, effort, attention, and money will be diverted toward developing a better relationship for the next 21 days. Trust me when I say the rewards far outweigh the costs. You are worth it, and so is your spouse.

Scott Simmerok, Senior Pastor
Church on the Hill, San Jose, California

Acknowledgments

To our son, Justen Hunter, my favorite writer and the teller of all good stories (even if the endings don't always turn out that way). You inspire me with your imagination and humor every day.

To our daughter, Kimberly Hunter, for again letting me get away with trying to be a mom and write a book at the same time. You are more fun every single day, and I am so glad that I not only get to be your mom, but also your friend.

To our daughter, Amanda. You're the kind of kid that parents hope for. Your maturity and beauty grow every single day.

To our son, Jeremy, whose determination and endurance in running are an inspiration to me in writing. I figure if you can run six miles in the rain, surely I can write two more pages.

To Roger's parents, Betty Dobson and Dewayne Lipp, who show us, the next generation, how to love on purpose.

To my group of girls, especially Kim Gonsalves, Angela Bowen, Vikki Francis, Shannon Jordahl, Denise Gaggins, Cindy Anderson, Kelly Simmerok, Tonya Walter, Lynette Furstenberg, Dina Garcia, Susy Flory and Cheri Gregory for your almost constant love, support, encouraging emails, and prayers.

To the team at Harvest House Publishers, including Barb Sherrill, who has held my hand through much of this book, as well as my editor-extraordinaire, Rod Morris, for letting me write like I talk and helping it all make sense in the end.

To Rachelle Gardner. You became an agent at the same time I became a writer. I, and many other writers, owe you a debt of gratitude for guiding all of us on how to navigate the beast known as publishing. The Christian publishing world is much better for having you in it.

To our friends at Church on the Hill in San Jose, California, with a special shout out to Pastor Scott Simmerok and Lisa Akin.

To Cathi Miller. Your contribution to this project will help an untold number of couples realize that each relationship is unique and worthy of attention. Your honesty is an inspiration.

And, once again, all the credit for getting this book done goes to *Teresa Drake*. They say the sophomore book is the hardest to write. I know that no one in the world hopes that is true more than you and I do. You are not only motivating and creative, but you are blessing the lives of many, many people in your ministry.

Laying a Foundation:

Preparing for *Happy Habits for Every Couple*

1

Why *Happy Habits*?

"With every deed you are sowing a seed,
though the harvest you may not see."
ELLA WHEELER WILCOX

I (Kathi) have a shelf full of marriage books, and I bet if you've been married for any amount of time, you do too.

Most of the books that I own are great books. They talk about God's desire for a healthy marriage, the theories behind a healthy marriage, and what a healthy marriage should look like if you apply these principles.

Some of those marriage books have had a great impact on my relationship with my husband.

Most of them? They ended up on our bookshelf as things I feel guilty for 1) not implementing daily and 2) not dusting.

When Roger and I got married we both brought two teenagers, a full-time job, and a host of volunteer activities into the relationship. There just wasn't much time to be sitting up in bed after a long day, taking turns reading pages out of marriage enhancement books and staring longingly, with great resolve, into each other's eyes.

On the other hand, Roger and I were determined to make this marriage work. We each had been in marriages that ended in divorce, and we were committed to do everything we could, in God's power, to see that we had a marriage that not only lasted, but also was honoring to Him and filled with joy.

That's when the crazy ideas started to flow.

First, there was *The Husband Project*, where I challenged my friends (and myself) to bless our men for 21 days without expecting anything in return. While most women kept it a secret from their husbands, I had to tell Roger eventually (he had a right to know what book I was working on seven hours a day).

> I gleaned the very best advice from every marriage book on our shelves and adapted it into short, doable projects we could work on together.

After that, Roger and I wanted a project to complete as a couple. The results of that are what you hold in your hand.

I wanted a way to bless my marriage that was practical, fun (and perhaps just a little bit flirty), and that followed God's plan and purpose for marriage. I needed something that wasn't just a theory about what to do about my marriage—I wanted some checkboxes. I wanted something that would instruct me, "This is what you do, now go and do it."

That is what I needed, and that is what I ended up writing.

Becoming an Expert on Your Own Marriage

I'm definitely not a marriage expert. After one failed marriage and just ten years into my second one, I'm probably not the first person you'd approach for marital advice. Although the fact that Roger and I got married with four teenagers between us, and we're still together, should earn us some kind of presidential Medal of Honor. Or at least a nifty certificate in a leatherette case.

So I gleaned and condensed the very best advice from every marriage book on our shelves and adapted it into short, doable steps or projects we could work on together.

This is how I have to manage almost every area of my life, whether it's healthy eating, child rearing, Bible study, or most recently, marriage.

It's not enough that I *know* what I'm supposed to do; I need to have a *plan* to get up and do it.

Through these crazy little projects (most taking less than five or ten minutes), my husband and I learned new things about each other. We rediscovered what makes each other tick, confirmed some basics we already knew, and found new and exciting ways to encourage one another. While I may not be a marriage expert, I became an expert on my marriage.

I love how *The Message* translates the words of James about putting feet to our thoughts:

> Dear friends, do you think you'll get anywhere in this if you learn all the right words but never do anything? Does merely talking about faith indicate that a person really has it? For instance, you come upon an old friend dressed in rags and half-starved and say, "Good morning, friend! Be clothed in Christ! Be filled with the Holy Spirit!" and walk off without providing so much as a coat or a cup of soup—where does that get you? Isn't it obvious that God-talk without God-acts is outrageous nonsense? (James 2:14-17 MSG)

We can talk about marriage all day long. We can buy books and listen to podcasts about how we should have great marriages. We can listen to sermons and do Bible studies. But unless we put some God-acts to our God-talk, no one benefits.

Thousands of couples have done the projects before you. These simple acts have been proven to change not only people's behavior, but also their attitudes. I pray that God pours out His blessings on you and your marriage as you put feet to His plan for your relationship.

2

Being Married on Purpose

"Change is inevitable, growth is intentional."
AUTHOR UNKNOWN

Before Roger and I got married, we had long conversations about what we wanted our marriage to look like. We both had plenty of examples in our lives of other couples' marriages—some of them we wanted to emulate; some we wanted to avoid.

With both of us heading into our second marriage, it was exciting to dream about what this marriage was going to look like. "This time," we told ourselves, "it's going to be different."

And while a lot of things were different, some things were remarkably familiar. Even though I was married to a different man, many of my same insecurities and fears were very present holdovers from my first marriage. Financial strains and our teenagers' angst hadn't magically disappeared in this new marriage (but instead of each of us having two teenagers, now we each had two teenagers and two stepkids).

I had been told over and over that this second marriage was going to be hard. But I guess I secretly hoped we would be the couple that escaped all the drama.

Shocking, I know, but we were not that lucky couple.

Oh, I know annoying things will always happen, but when the toilet overflows, someone in the house gets the flu (again), or the bank sends a friendly note letting us know they happily covered our banking miscalculation (for a nominal fee close to what it costs to feed six at the Golden Arches), I get overly panicked, frustrated, and mad.

It was also a great surprise after three weeks of marriage to discover that those heart palpitations and overwhelming feelings of desperate love were not enough to cover the fact that no one in my new blended family shared my passion to have a sink that wasn't loaded with enough dishes to fill our cupboards.

God's Word tells us not only to expect the good, the bad, and the ugly but also that it comes from or is allowed by Him. We don't always understand the trials, but we can trust the One who sent them.

> When times are good, be happy;
>   but when times are bad, consider this:
> God has made the one
>   as well as the other.
>   (Ecclesiastes 7:14)

About six months into our marriage, I remember Roger and I looking at each other and saying out loud, "What have we gotten ourselves into?" This wasn't the marriage we had dreamed about. Life was just as stressful as when I was single, but now I had to take into consideration another person's moods and opinions.

> We determined that if we wanted to make this marriage work, we had to be intentional in everything we did.

And yes, I'm sure Roger would admit to reflecting with some longing on his bachelor days.

After long, heated discussions and a river of tears on my part, we knew we needed to make some changes, fast, if we didn't want this marriage to go the same way as our firsts.

It was about that time that Roger came up with the watchword for our marriage: *intentional.*

We determined that if we wanted to make this marriage work, we had to be intentional in everything we did. We would be intentional about inviting God into our marriage each day. We would be intentional about our time spent together and the conversations we shared. We would be intentional about supporting each other and looking for the good in each other, instead of constantly recognizing what was driving us nuts.

No, it doesn't always work out perfectly. And yes, we fight and we bicker and we say stupid things. But we have a standard for our marriage, one we can hold each other to in the most stressful times. That standard is to intentionally discover the best in our partner, every day.

Seeing Your Spouse Through New Eyes

The report we overwhelmingly heard over and over from the initial participants in *Happy Habits for Every Couple* was that a lot of things changed for each couple. Some people realized they were putting all their energy and focus into their kids and careers, while giving the meager leftovers to their husband or wife. Some couples realized they had already established some pretty great habits in their marriage, and doing the projects affirmed and reinforced what they had learned over the years: It takes a lot of hard work to have a great marriage.

But by far the realization that most of the original project participants walked away with was this: It wasn't so much that their spouse had changed over the course of their marriage, but *the way they viewed their spouse had changed considerably*.

Look at what my friend, speaker and author Cheri Gregory, said in a blog posting titled "A Healthy Marriage Majors in History (not Math)" about being intentional in the way you see your spouse and your marriage:

> Think about a high school math class: What does the teacher put on the board every day? **Problems!** What is the math textbook filled with? **Problems!** What do students have for homework each night? **Problems!**
>
> And what is the goal with all these problems? **Solve them!**
>
> In contrast, think about a high school history class. What does the teacher discuss in class? **Facts!** What is the history

textbook filled with? **Facts!** What do students memorize in preparation for quizzes? **Facts!**

And how do we approach history facts? Do we try to somehow "solve" them? Do we try to change Independence Day from July 4 to, say, May 28? Of course not. We know that we can't "solve" facts. When it comes to facts, our goal is to accept them, understand them, and learn from them.

So why do I say that a healthy marriage majors in history, not math?

Because no matter how I may be feeling at the moment, my husband is never "a problem"! He does not need me to "solve" him. "Math mode" simply does not work for marriage.

History habits, on the other hand, strengthen marriage. My husband is a living, breathing, walking, talking collection of facts. And **he needs me to accept him, understand him,** and **learn from him** rather than fix him.

Exactly what do "history habits" look like in day-to-day living?

Back when Daniel and I were dating, I was an expert at "history habits." I focused on my beloved's strengths and liberally exercised my bragging rights, telling everyone what he was famous for.

Once we married, however, I quickly slipped into "math mode." Whenever things didn't go the way I wanted, I switched to critical thinking, focusing on my husband's weaknesses, trying harder and harder to "solve" the problem (as I perceived it): him!

The difference between "history habits" and "math mode" is simply a matter of focus. When I'm practicing "history habits," I'm focused on my husband's strengths. When I fall into "math mode," I'm focused on my husband's weaknesses, trying desperately to "solve" someone I once vowed to accept.

When your spouse doesn't respond in the way you expect to all the project work you've done, when you're cranky and the last thing you want to do is anything with the word *Bonus* in it, remember, this is your opportunity to be intentional about seeing your spouse—and your marriage—in a new way.

3

A Quick How-To Guide

Here is your step-by-step guide to getting the most out of this book:

1. Start with the prep week.

This is the week before you start the 21 projects. Use this week to complete the items below. Also, take a look at the *Prep Week Checklist* (found on page 38) to ensure you're fully prepared to start the projects.

2. Read through all the projects.

This is your chance to get a feel for all 21 projects. Be sure to use this entire book—make notes in the margins, scribble and doodle on the pages, and start to think about ways to tailor each project to your spouse.

3. Find another couple who wants to work through *Happy Habits for Every Couple* with you and will encourage you and hold you accountable.

It doesn't matter if they're phone friends, Internet buddies, or face-to-face friends you meet with at Starbucks down the street. Location is not important; consistency is. Figure out a time to spend together (after everyone has read through the book) to come up with a plan for when and how you're going to do the projects.

4. Sign *"Happy Habits for Every Couple* Encouragement Covenant."

You can find this on page 43.

5. Decide on a start date.

If you're doing this with other couples (as a small group or as a church), someone has probably decided on a start date for you. If not, now is the time to make that decision. Mark it in bold on your calendar and set up an email reminder on your computer.

6. Look over the daily projects together and come up with a plan.

As a couple, decide how you'll bless your marriage each day. I've provided a variety of ideas, but it's up to you to decide how you'll carry out each day's project. Get creative and come up with a new and wonderful way to make your marriage rock.

In the space provided under each project, write down in advance what you're going to do for each day.

You'll also need to make some specific plans along the way. Is there a night when you'll need babysitting? Get on the phone now. Is there a special candy you can purchase only online and need to order now for next Saturday's project? Order it in advance so you'll be ready.

7. Share your project plan with your accountability partners.

We recommend that you make copies of your calendar to share with your accountability partners (you'll find the "Project Planner" on page 215). That way, you can commit to pray for each other, as well as lend support on days that may be particularly challenging. Who knows, your partners may have some great, creative ideas to share.

8. Be flexible.

If one of the projects doesn't line up with your schedule, swap it for another day. If food does nothing for your husband, find another way to treat him. This is all about connecting with your man. If your wife hates gushy cards, find one that's fun and flattering all at the same time. The purpose of *Happy Habits for Every Couple* is not to make you crazy, but to help you find new ways to bless and support your marriage. Just do *something* intentionally every day to accomplish that goal.

4

Why 21 Days?

If 21 days seems like an arbitrary amount of time, let me explain the method to my madness.

We've all heard the old adage that it takes 21 days to either make or break a habit, and I've found this to be true in many areas of my life. Whether it's food or exercise, nail biting or Bible reading, 21 days seems to be a magic number for either creating or breaking habits.

But I also want to give you an amount of time that is both life changing and doable.

I tend to be an outgoing person, but I dislike any type of crowd. I can grow anxious just thinking about visiting my local Target or going to Home Depot to pick up a plant. I hate lines, I hate crowds.

One time when I described this feeling to my friend James, I said, "I feel like when I go out into the world, I'm just holding my breath until I do what I have to do and can get home to my chair and my DVR."

Instead of him being shocked by my revelation, I found a fellow anxiety freak.

I think for 21 days, we can all do this together.

"Absolutely, I totally get it," he said. "I'm very annoyed when anything has to be done away from my house. I've got my wife, my dogs, and my high-def big screen. Why would I want to leave the house?"

Ah, my fellow agoraphobics unite!

Some of the things I'm going to ask you to do in *Happy Habits for Every Couple* are going to feel uncomfortable, outside of what feels safe and secure. You're going to have to talk about things you may have never talked about, you may have to do something you've never done before, and I totally understand that this will be outside of your comfort zone.

But I think we can all "hold our breath" for 21 days. You have a week up front to prepare, and then just 21 days of being on "project status." Just 21 days of diverting your time and energy and money to your marriage. It's going to be inconvenient. It's going to bump up against other things on your calendar.

But I think for 21 days, we can all do this together.

5

Prepping for the Projects

"Organizing is what you do before you do something,
so that when you do it, it is not all mixed up."

A.A. MILNE

My hope for you is that you'll make it through all 21 days of projects. None of the projects are complicated or difficult, but unless you have a plan that you talk about and agree upon with your spouse, life will get in the way of your best intentions.

Communication—A Great Way to Save You from Misunderstandings (and Potential Public Embarrassment)

Several years ago, I visited a church where it was evident that when it came to synergy in the Sunday morning worship service, this team had it down. After an amazing time of worship through music, we were spellbound by a pastor who was a gifted preacher. His sermon was all about how a shepherd has to watch his sheep closely because, left to their own devices, sheep can get into a whole mess of trouble. Throughout the sermon, the pastor kept talking about just how cosmically dumb sheep are, providing great illustrations along the way. The beginning worship was great, the sermon was great. And then it happened.

At the end of the sermon, it was time to respond in worship with some singing. The selected hymn? "Lamb of God." (No, I'm not kidding.)

It's obvious what had happened. The pastor told the worship director his sermon topic; it was going to be about sheep. Worship director thinks, *Hmmmm, sheep...lamb...I know, "Lamb of God"!*

Everyone had the best of intentions, but it wasn't the worshipful moment I'm sure the leadership team intended.

> It's critical that you and your spouse carve out a week specifically for creating a plan for each project.

Planning for Success

I want you to have success with *Happy Habits for Every Couple*, which is why it's critical that you and your spouse carve out a week specifically for creating a plan for each project. (Yes, an entire week so you have enough time to make plans that sizzle, not just fill up the page.)

Here's a checklist of things to think about as you prep for the projects:

Prep Week Checklist

- Have we put the Major Projects on the calendar?
- Have we put the Bonus Projects on the calendar?
- Have we looked at our individual calendars and our family calendar to see what obstacles may come up?
- Do we need to plan for babysitters for the Major Projects or Bonus Projects?
- Have the guys gotten together to plan the double date?
- Is there a special treat I want to buy or order off the Internet for one of the projects?
- Do we need to make reservations for one of the Major Projects?

By investing your time on the front end, you'll have a plan that you both agree upon, which will reduce fighting and crossed expectations (a win for everyone) and give you a much greater chance for satisfaction and success.

6

Creating Your Encouragement Crew

*"Taking an interest in what others are thinking
and doing is often a much more powerful
form of encouragement than praise."*

Robert Martin

I want you and your partner to succeed with *Happy Habits for Every Couple*. I want you to get all the benefits you can from this book and your time together. I don't want this to be another book that you put on your shelf and think, *Oh yeah, I remember that book. I guess I'll just donate it to Goodwill along with our collection of Atkins cookbooks and our VHS tapes from that weird Tae Bo phase.*

Don't get swallowed up by good intentions and then kick yourself when there's no follow through (says the woman with three unopened *Walk Praise!* CDs). I want this to be a book you use and receive every benefit that God has waiting for you and your sweetheart.

That's why you need to get your encouragement crew in place.

Call them what you will, these are the people who will pester you when you become too busy to do the projects. These are the people who will check on you to make sure your

> These are the people who will remind you why you need to do the projects when you just don't feel like it.

dates are planned. These are the people who will have very awkward conversations with you about Bonus Projects.

Most importantly, these are the people who will remind you why you need to do the projects when you just don't feel like it.

In a former life, I spent several years as a sales rep in the gift industry. While my main job was peddling stuffed teddy bears and scented candles to drugstore chains, several times a year I would get together with other sales reps from around the state for meetings.

My sales manager, Michael, had been part of the gift industry for years. While he was not what you would call cheap, part of the reason he was a successful businessman was that he watched the bottom line. He was always very careful to get the best deal he could and negotiated in every situation I had ever seen him in.

We were out to lunch one day, discussing where he would hold our next annual sales meeting. Usually it was at a hotel off the beach in Santa Cruz, California (our annual meetings were held in December and qualified for the off-season rate), so I was surprised he was considering other locations.

"You mean we aren't going to Santa Cruz?" I said. "I thought that was the cheapest, I mean, most cost-effective solution?"

"Oh, we're probably going back there, but that's by no means the best deal financially," Michael said.

I was surprised. "So where would be the cheapest?"

"Reno would be a much better option. It's more centrally located for all the sales reps, they practically give away hotel and meeting rooms, and food is reasonably priced. I could probably do the meeting for two-thirds or half the cost of doing it in Santa Cruz."

My bags were practically packed. Snow? Shopping? Mountains? Shopping? Sign me up. I'm much more of a snow bear than a beach bunny.

"So Michael, let's do it! I think it's a great idea." I was ready to roll. Too bad it was only June.

"Nope, no can do. Yes, it would save a lot of money. I'm just worried about a couple of our sales reps. I know that one has a serious gambling problem, and the other seems to be developing one. I just can't in good conscience put them up at a hotel with a gambling floor in the lobby." Michael sighed and moved the conversation to the new line of coffee-scented candles we were repping.

Michael had every right to make the best business decision for his company, the cost-effective decision to meet in Reno. Instead, he set aside personal convenience and department profits in order to support two people he cared about.

This powerful example has stuck with me for years. Sometimes loving and supporting others can be extremely inconvenient and costly, but it's essential if we want to become part of a community of healthy, growing Christ-followers. We need people to cheer us on as we make radical Christ-obedient decisions, and we need people who will point out the hazards ahead if we choose to go our own way.

> You need to be part of a community that will love you and cheer you to the finish line.

For *Happy Habits for Every Couple* to have any lasting effect, you need to be part of a community that will love you and cheer you to the finish line.

That's why whether you're doing this on your own as a couple or with a larger group, you must bring another couple on board to cheer you on. Make sure they're partners who will speak the truth to you in love. You want truth tellers in your life, but truth tellers that are committed to loving you and seeing you grow.

Once you've found those people to cheer you on (and check up on you) read over and commit to the "*Happy Habits for Every Couple* Encouragement Covenant" found on page 43. This will mean putting aside a little time to touch base with each other and be there if issues arise, but won't it be great knowing someone else has your back as well?

Happy Habits for Every Couple
Encouragement Covenant

The Covenant

We, the readers of *Happy Habits for Every Couple*, enthusiastically agree to enter into an encouraging relationship with each other for the sole purpose of engaging in and completing all projects to intentionally love and support our spouse. As the encouragement crew we vow to:

- Encourage each person in our crew
- Check in with each other at least once a week
- Put our plans on paper and discuss them with each other
- Laugh only *with* each other, not *at* each other
- Not talk badly about our spouse for the 21 days
- Pray for each other every day for the 21 days
- Keep details confidential. What we discuss with our encouragement crew stays with our encouragement crew
- Ask for help, motivation, or inspiration if we're having a rough time with any part of the projects

We the undersigned acknowledge and agree to the terms of the *Happy Habits for Every Couple* Encouragement Covenant on this

___ day of _____, 20__.

_____

Project Manager (Husband)

_____

Project Manager (Wife)

_____

Encourager

_____

Encourager

You can download a copy here: http://www.kathilipp.com/happyhabits /downloads/EncouragementCovenant

7

How to Handle Tough Situations During the Projects

ere are some of the common issues people raise when it comes to the projects:

We just don't have time for all this stuff.

I understand that life is beyond busy. There are jobs, there are kids, there's a house to maintain, a church that needs volunteers—oh, and there's that whole sleep thing that seems totally negotiable much of the time so you can just keep the basics of life going.

Several years ago, our kids, Amanda and Jeremy, were white-water rafting down the Russian River near Sacramento. Several kids were on the trip, ranging in ages from the youngest at 10 to Jeremy, who was 17. Amanda, at 18, was along as a chaperone.

At one point on the trip, the raft hit white water, tossing all the passengers into the river. The guide, used to rough waters, stayed dry inside the raft. As Amanda and Jeremy scrambled to gather up all the littlest passengers and get them into the boat, the guide told them, "No, adults go in first." This surprised Amanda and Jeremy, but they obediently got onto the raft first. "If you spend all of your energy putting those wet, wiggly kids into the boat, you won't have enough energy to get yourself into the raft. You have to get into the boat first." Once they were in the boat, it became easier to help the younger kids into the boat, bringing everyone to safety.

When the situation warrants, you must be willing to get into the boat first. Yes, your kids need your time and attention. Yes, you must do your best at work while you're there. But if you don't commit time to taking care of your marriage, not only are you missing out on the joys that a healthy Christ-centered relationship brings, your kids are missing out on the benefits of having parents who are crazy about each other. (Besides, what's the fun of having kids if you can't embarrass them by making out at the mall when they are around?)

With the cost of babysitting, movies, and dinner, we can't afford to go out.

Every time there's a sermon at church about finances, something is usually said about how money is wasted.

Ever hear of the "*Latte* Factor"? This example is trotted out to show how much money we're wasting and, hence, how much we could save if we'd just stop drinking those evil lattes. Simply multiply the number of lattes purchased at Starbucks each year (my personal number: 100+) by the cost of the latte ($4.25 with the really yummy extra shot of sugar-free vanilla) and that amount could:

- send three extra teens to summer camp (getting them out of their parents' hair, which is a worthy cause)
- pay off a credit card debt
- remodel a small kitchen
- settle the national debt for a third-world country

Yes, I agree we need a plan for our money (John Maxwell said, "A budget is telling your money where to go instead of wondering where it went"), but can we spread the blame a little when it comes to financial finger pointing?

I want to see the sermon on the "*Best Buy* Factor" or the "*Cable Television So We Can Have ESPN* Factor" or "*Having Your Children in Tap, Ballet, Soccer, and Kids Cooking Class All in the Same Week* Factor." Leave my coffee out of this.

Besides, those lattes help keep peace in my marriage. (Let's just say that things could get real ugly around this house if Mama don't get her joe.)

But the facts are indisputable. It's not usually that we don't have enough money for the things that are important; it's that we choose to spend our money in less important ways leaving not enough money for the truly important things—like working on our marriage.

And my marriage—your marriage— deserves better than leftovers.

> My marriage— your marriage— deserves better than leftovers.

Because this is a project—a short period of time where you focus your time, energy, and resources on one goal—I ask you to put your budget on project status as well.

What if my spouse doesn't want to do the projects?

I know it can be frustrating to go it alone. You imagine other couples lounging in bed, snuggling together in a cloud of fluffy pillows, whispering sweet nothings into each other's ears as they read their lists of why they love each other so much. And it makes you want to gag a little. Okay, maybe a lot.

But I think you should still do the projects. Let me explain.

Every year I participate in the Willow Creek Leadership Conference. Every August, thousands of people attend this amazing event on Willow Creek's campus in Barrington, Illinois. But for leaders from churches faraway, like ours, smack dab in the heart of Silicon Valley, attendance can be costly and time prohibitive.

Years ago, Willow Creek got the idea to take the conference off campus and do satellite feeds to several churches—not just around the country but around the world. I can't imagine the logistics that go into making that happen. Between language barriers, time zone differences, and satellite issues, the moving parts on that process are overwhelming.

Since we're in California, and the conference originates from Chicago, we spend our day watching a Jumbotron displaying events that happened two hours earlier on the stage at Willow Creek.

The people who produce the event do everything in their power to make sure we all feel like we're part of the action. The speakers talk to the satellite sites as if they were sitting in the room. Everything is timed to the second for a seamless appearance. But even with all that, you can't help but notice that it's a satellite broadcast.

> This is about doing what God has designed you to do even when it feels as if it's having no effect on your spouse... because it's having an effect on you.

Last year, many sites lost their video feed due to extreme weather conditions. This year, despite heroic efforts from the technical team, the audio and video were so far out of sync that we spent much of the two days feeling as if we were watching a bad Godzilla movie.

Everyone watching in California knows that what we're seeing happened two hours earlier—it's no big secret. But when the worship leader appears on the screen to lead worship, we all respond. When the speaker shares a great illustration, we all laugh and clap as if he were in our pulpit on a Sunday morning.

We all respond, not because the speaker needs to hear it or because the band needs to know we're with them. We respond because we're designed that way. Even if there's no one on the other end to hear our laughter, we need to laugh. Even if the speaker never hears our applause at the end of her speech, we need to express our joy and gratitude at what we've heard.

I understand many of you are going into this with a spouse that is, well, let's just say less than enthused. Not everyone will begin with a sense of dedication and commitment.

So why go through the projects if you're the only one doing them?

Because it's not just for your spouse, it's for you and your marriage. Plus, it's an act of worship. Every act of obedience is an act of worship.

Even if our spouses don't participate, even if they don't act the way we'd like them to, we need to be the people who keep working it out, because we need it.

This isn't just about what *we* can do in our marriages. It's about what *God* can do when we obey, even when it doesn't seem to make a difference. It's about practicing good habits when the easy thing to do would be to go and watch TV. It's about loving our spouses when they're not lovable and when we don't feel loving.

It's about doing what God has designed you to do even when it feels as if it's having no effect on your spouse...because it's having an effect on you, as this recent project participant attests:

> When you came and spoke, my husband and I were going through some very difficult times. We even separated for a little while. At the time I started the projects, there was still residual bitterness about a lot of issues because our reconciliation was more out of honoring our obligations than it was a heartfelt, romantic inspiration to be with each other.
>
> Some of these projects were incredibly hard for me, and I did them very begrudgingly, especially the ones where you thank him for specific things you admire/appreciate about him, notice good things, or give him time. I didn't feel those things about him, but more importantly I didn't feel he deserved them. But I did them. And I found those little gestures helped soften the bitterness and distrust that was between us. It opened up opportunities for more reconciliation.
>
> Sometimes your spouse just needs to know you're on their side. For me, the projects put me on that side, because I wasn't there to begin with. As I saw him responding, it really helped me to see how desperately he needed to know I believed in him, and believed he was valuable.
>
> We still have some huge problems, and God has done some

great things in bringing other people into his life that can help our serious marriage problems. I'm going through and doing the projects again, but not so bitterly this time!—Julie

So go ahead and do the projects—even if you're not getting any cooperation or response. On the days when you're supposed to do the projects together, you can either (1) find a way to serve your spouse that is similar to the project or (2) take some time to care for yourself in a way that you may not normally.

What if I'm traveling? What if my partner is traveling? What if one of us is sick? Should we keep doing the projects?

This is your call, but I encourage you to do what you can. Many couples have done projects while they've been apart. When your husband is on a golf trip, you can still write down 12 things you respect about him. When your wife is in Tulsa at a sales convention, you can still clean out the vegetable drawers of the fridge. For the projects that require you to be physically present, you can either modify the project or swap it for another date.

As far as being sick, here was our yardstick for whether to skip the project or soldier through: If we were well enough to go to work, we were well enough to do the project. (And remember, sometimes the most romantic thing you can do is make sure the bucket is within arm's length of the one you love.)

8

Planning for Those
Barry White Moments

An Introduction to Bonus Projects

*"Anybody who believes that the way to a man's heart
is through his stomach flunked geography."*

ROBERT BYRNE

I n my first book, *The Husband Project*, one of the weekly projects
was to have sex with your husband. (And yes, I have heard of
several men who obtained a copy of the book and laid it in a strategic
location for their wives.)

There was a lot of good-natured grumbling and some outright
hostility about those projects, but I stand by them. In a healthy marriage—barring physical issues—sex is one of the most important and
necessary ingredients.

So it was refreshing to receive this email from a friend who was
doing *The Husband Project* with a group of women at her church:

> Hey Kath,
>
> I cannot thank you enough for the projects. They really have
> made a difference for my husband and me (he still doesn't
> know I'm doing the book, but he's just glad something is
> going on!).
>
> The thing that really has surprised me the most was to under-
> stand some of my "issues" around the Bonus Projects. I know

you said to aim for early in the week so if things came up, I could still get those done. Well, I kept putting them off until my accountability partner asked if I had done it. I knew it had to be tonight or I wouldn't have done it within the week. (My accountability partners and I had agreed to get each other massages if we completed *all* the projects, and you know how much I love a good massage!)

> "Some people would think, 'How unromantic, planning for sex,' but I have discovered that is exactly what I need."

But something interesting happened. As soon as I started planning to have sex with Matt, the more excited I got about it. I called him at work and flirted a little. I changed the sheets on the bed and made sure I put on the good lotion after my shower. I even shaved my legs (now that's love!).

I had forgotten what it was like to be excited about having sex. Oh yeah, while we were engaged, that was all we talked about—when we would get to. But I have to be honest, until the projects, I haven't been looking forward to it. It just seems like one more thing I have to do. That's not Matt's fault. I love him deeply, but I am just realizing that I need a plan.

I know some people would think, "How unromantic, planning for sex," but I think I have discovered that is exactly what I need.   —Trish

That is why I want you to plan for sex. There's a special thrill that comes from knowing that you and your spouse are doing something special, just the two of you, and preparing for it.

Some of the Ways You Can Prepare

- Flirt on the phone with your honey throughout the day.
- Break out the body lotion or massage oil and leave it on the nightstand.
- Pull together an iPod list of romantic songs.
- Mist your bedsheets with lavender spray.
- Take a long, hot scented bath.
- Put a few snacks and some bottled water in your bedroom (for endurance).
- Take a shower (together or alone).

And If You're Not Looking Forward to It?

Yes, there are just times when it's not going to be convenient, when you're tired, and when you just don't want to (for women and men). Here's the advice I was given as a newlywed: If your spouse is in the mood and you're not, ask him or her to wait a couple of minutes. Go into the bathroom and prepare yourself and pray. Take a shower and ask God to give you the heart that you need at the moment.

Something remarkable happens when you take a couple of minutes to prepare, pray, and refocus. I can't guarantee it for everyone, but it's a strategy that many of my friends and I use, and it works.

The Why and How of a Great Sex Life

In a recent daytime talk show, the resident health guru was answering questions about men's health. A gentleman from the audience approached the microphone, knowing that wives were listening in a separate room, and asked the doctor the one question every man in the room wanted to know the answer to: "How many times a week should a man have sex?"

The doctor's reply? "For optimal health, a man should be having sex four times a week."

Four times a week! I couldn't believe it. My first thought was, *OK, this doctor has been sniffing a little too much antibacterial hand cleaner.* But then I became convicted. Putting aside my own selfishness, I really did want to make sure that I was doing everything I could for my husband's health.

So I bought him a treadmill.

OK, not really. But I have to admit that little piece of information, whether this doctor knew what he was talking about or not, did make me think about sex in a whole new way.

> Most couples are a mismatch when it comes to sexual appetite. God's Word is clear about how we're to handle that.

Now regarding the questions you asked in your letter. Yes, it is good to abstain from sexual relations. But because there is so much sexual immorality, each man should have his own wife, and each woman should have her own husband.

The husband should fulfill his wife's sexual needs, and the wife should fulfill her husband's needs. The wife gives authority over her body to her husband, and the husband gives authority over his body to his wife (1 Corinthians 7:1-4 NLT).

Yep, it's one of the most quoted passages in the Bible. And it's clear. We don't get to have sex only when we feel like it or when it's convenient. We need to make every attempt to grow this area of our relationship in healthy and mutually agreeable ways.

So whether we're motivated to or not, we've got to spend some energy to figure out this sex thing.

I don't have the expertise to go into the whys and hows of marital sex. (At the end of this chapter you'll find a list of books and marriage conferences by authors and speakers who are experts in this area, if you're inclined to investigate further.) My purpose in the Bonus Projects is to give you some fun and creative ideas to make sex happen on a weekly—or more often, I hope—basis.

Starting the Conversation

The first step toward a great sex life is great communication. Each of us is responsible for encouraging open and honest dialogue about the amount of physical intimacy happening in our marriage. If both partners are determined to serve each other in this area, there can be grace, passion, enjoyment, and in some cases healing in this very important part of our relationship.

> Each of us is responsible for encouraging open and honest dialogue about the amount of physical intimacy happening in our marriage.

Consider reading a book or two and looking into other appropriate resources regarding sex in marriage, and then share your findings or ideas with your spouse. I've noticed in my own marriage that when things seem to have cooled down in this area that the absolute best ways for me to "freshen things up" are to:

- talk with my husband about sex and how we're doing in that department
- read about how to make our sex life more fulfilling and passionate for the both of us

Could you think of a better homework project? Here's how to put those ideas into practice:

1. Talk about sex with your partner.

Every couple should have a standing date night—a night away from the kids, away from the house and responsibilities. This would be an excellent place to talk, at least once a month, about where you are as a couple with your sex life.

If being away from the house is the best place to talk about sex, where is the worst place? The bedroom.

Never, ever, talk about your sex life right before or after having sex. Before is way too stressful, especially if one of the partners is trying to share from the heart and the other one has the obvious air of: "Yeah, yeah, yeah, blah, blah, blah. Less talk and more action please."

On the other hand, talking about sex right after having it gives the distinct impression that you're judging what just took place. No one needs to feel like a gymnast at the Summer Games who's just been given a low score for a sloppy dismount.

2. Bring in the big guns and listen to the experts.

Check out these great resources on marriage and sex to help you with your homework:

Books

For Men Only: A Straightforward Guide to the Inner Lives of Women by Shaunti Feldhahn and Jeff Feldhahn

For Women Only: What You Need to Know about the Inner Lives of Men by Shaunti Feldhahn

Intended for Pleasure: Sex Technique and Sexual Fulfillment in Christian Marriage (fourth edition) by Ed Wheat and Gaye Wheat

Intimate Issues: 21 Questions Christian Women Ask About Sex by Linda Dillow and Lorraine Pintus

Red-Hot Monogamy: Making Your Marriage Sizzle by Bill Farrel and Pam Farrel

Sex Begins in the Kitchen: Creating Intimacy to Make Your Marriage Sizzle by Kevin Leman

Sheet Music: Uncovering the Secrets of Sexual Intimacy in Marriage by Kevin Leman

When Two Become One: Enhancing Sexual Intimacy in Marriage by
   Christopher and Rachel McCluskey
The Good Girl's Guide to Great Sex by Sheila Wray Gregoire

Conferences

The Intimate Issues Conference for Women (www.intimateissues.com)

The Weekend to Remember Conference (www.familylife.com)

9

Learning to Date Again
An Introduction to the Major Projects

Of all the projects, the ones I'm calling Major Projects got the most resistance from my test group. I could not believe how many couples thought it was inconceivable to go on a date with their partner.

Yes, I know that babysitting is expensive.

Yes, I know that traditional dating is expensive.

Yes, I know that you don't like the same movies.

Yes, I know that at the end of the week you are exhausted.

I want you to date anyway.

For the next three weeks, have one date a week. And whatever your challenge—babysitting, money, time—be creative and make it work. I have listed below some ideas to get you started:

Guy-Centric Dates
Action and Adventure Dates

The first two suggestions are from my pastor, Scott:

1. This is the best all-time cool date that my wife ever suggested. This one leaves all the other guys longing to be married to my wife. I shared this in church six months ago and got a lot of feedback from guys about how cool that was, and some wives even did this for their husbands. Kelli

suggested we go to the shooting range and shoot pistols. It was an indoor range where you could rent guns. It's the manliest date I've ever been on. Combine that with a red-meat dinner and top it off with a little sex (or a lot of sex), and there you have the perfect night! No one will be able to top that.

2. Another date that I've wanted to try is a wind tunnel where you simulate sky-diving. It's a good date as long as the girl doesn't mind messing up her hair.

Here are some additional ideas from Doug:

1. A bucket of balls at the driving range

2. Go-kart racing at an enclosed course

3. Strings-attached massage (enough said)

4. Playing Rock Band on the Wii or some other video game together

5. Paintballing (Skip says, "There is nothing sexier than a woman in camo.")

"I'm Not a Typical Guy" Dates

I had more than a few guys start off their list to me with the above statement. Apparently many men don't feel like "typical guys" if they don't chew tobacco and want to shoot things. Let me be the first to tell you, with so many men wanting less Matrix-style dating, you're in good company. Here are some great date ideas from the "Not a Typical Guy" set.

A few from Kevin:

1. I like to eat and my wife, Ruth, likes to cook, so we pick a recipe that sounds good (and date-worthy) and cook together.

2. I like to eat (wait, I said that already), so we just go out on

dinner dates. We dress up (me in Dockers and a polo shirt) to distinguish it from other times. I work at home and dress like a bum 98 percent of the time, so I like to dress up for some dates.

3. We've taken cooking classes together at a local kitchen-supply store.

4. I like plays, so we're on the email list of every local theater company and go to plays together.

5. Simple, at-home date night is watching an episode of either *Monk, Psych,* or *House,* which we have on DVD and both really like.

> "If a woman is planning a date night for her husband, she should let him in on the whole agenda."

A few from my husband, Roger:

1. Spend the evening working a puzzle. I know that I sound like I'm one step away from the retirement home, but it's actually a great way for us to do something and talk at the same time.

2. Get a coffee drink and hang out at a local bookstore.

3. Have a cookout at a day-use campground.

4. Go out for dessert without considering the calorie count and fat content of every bite.

Finally, my friend Kevin gave me the following piece of sage advice for women date planners everywhere:

> If a woman is planning a date night for her husband, she should let him in on the whole agenda. If the guy knows that tonight will or won't include sex, he will relax and enjoy the activity of dating. When he doesn't know, he may create a false expectation, which leads to a date-night disappointment—an unmet expectation (when the wife's goal was to

show love and perhaps be reciprocal in the dating process). This upfront honesty is also good, because a wife planning a date night doesn't have to limit her choices to only when she's "willing."

Girl-Centric Dates

Here are some great ideas from some of my best girls. Thanks to Kelli, Sherry, and Angela (you have some great husbands):

1. Purchase tickets for a concert (especially if it features a girl band circa 1984—go Bangles!).

2. Go on a less-than-strenuous hike and take a picnic lunch (he plans the hike and packs the lunch).

3. Plan and cook me dinner *and* do the dishes.

4. Get-up-and-go-get Starbucks, then go on a walking trail for a hike and talk along the way.

5. Go to the beach at sundown, listen to the waves, and watch the evening sun glisten on the water. A scrumptious dinner afterward is also very nice.

6. Go to Campo di Bocce (a local restaurant that also offers bocce ball). We've gone with another couple, played bocce, and then enjoyed dinner. Lots of fun!

7. Select a recipe from the Food Network website, shop for the ingredients at the fancy market in town, and then cook and eat.

8. Watch a chick flick accompanied by a foot massage. *Purrrrr.*

9. Go to a museum and eat at their café.

10. Take a full day to just drive and stop for lunch. It's the drive that counts as the activity, not just transportation to get there. (So no grumbling about whether we're "making good time" is allowed.)

11. Go to a major city and take in some window-shopping.

12. Dine at restaurants that don't have the menu in lights. No value meals, no happy meals, nothing with the word *meal* in it.

13. No strings attached massage.

Dating with Children

If you're married with kids, you might want to plan the occasional date that involves the whole family. Here are some ideas for inexpensive ways to make that happen.

1. *Drinking and Driving*—coffee that is. Roger and I love to drive-thru and grab hot drinks and take long drives at night. (Great date for people who have grown kids or kids small enough to fall asleep in the backseat of the car.)

2. *Carpet Picnic*—This one is great with younger kids. Give the kitchen table a rest and spread out some blankets (or plastic tablecloths depending on your kid's level of spillage). Put on a fun *Veggie Tales* movie and break out the yummy finger food. Soup is not recommended.

3. *Drive-in Movies*—The best idea here is to drive around with your toddlers in their car seats until they fall asleep; then you can make out during the movie. Another advantage is that you don't have to sneak in your store-bought candy; you can even bring a hibachi into the parking lot to cook dinner before the double feature. Since the number of drive-in theaters still operating has shrunk significantly over the past couple of decades, check out www.drive-ins.com for a current listing for your area.

4. *Mega Movies*—One of the nicer shopping areas in our town projects family-friendly movies onto the side of a building. People are encouraged to buy their dinner from one of the

local restaurants or bring a picnic. Lots of fun, low cost, and nobody minds if in the middle of the movie your kid needs a jumping break.

20 Dates for Less than $20

1. *Be a Tourist in Your Own Town*—Ask your friends for their favorite "cheap date" spots. See if your museum has a "First Sunday Free" program or some similar discount. For less than $20 you could do a free museum tour and actually afford to eat at their café.

2. *Coffee*—And not the drive-thru. Go in, order a couple of tall lattes, two giant cookies, and soak up all that atmosphere.

3. *Dive Dining*—Some of our favorite restaurants are holes-in-the-wall, never promoted in national advertising campaigns. We love to eat at a taqueria down the road from our church, the place with lumpia Filipino spring rolls on the east side of town, and the falafel stand next to the university. All of these places have amazing food for relatively cheap prices.

4. *Be a '50s Retro Couple*—Get together with another couple to play cards and have dessert. (Bonus points if you play bridge or canasta and drink Sanka.)

5. *Breakfast in Bed*—This date requires some planning the night before. Friday night grab a box of donuts or sweet rolls from a bakery and purchase the local paper at a newsstand. Set the timer on your coffeepot to go off midmorning Saturday. When the aroma of Starbucks' Sumatra Blend lures you from the sheets, put the paper, the rolls, and a pot of coffee on a tray and plan on lingering in bed. Who cares if you're reading yesterday's news? Enjoy the comics, the sports page, and the lifestyle section. If you have young kids, bring home enough rolls or donuts to share.

6. *You Light Up My Life*—During the holidays, looking at Christmas lights is our absolute favorite thing to do. Most local papers publish a guide to all the best displays in your city. Pack a thermos of peppermint hot chocolate and play your favorite Christmas CD to "make the spirits bright." You can even include the kids with this one.

7. *Music in the Park*—Many downtown associations offer Concerts in the Park throughout the warm and sunny seasons. Either pack a dinner or eat beforehand, and then enjoy a double scoop of ice cream on a waffle cone.

8. *Putt-Putt Golf*—Miniature golf may sound like the classic "getting to know you" first date (watching your fix-up throw his club at the mini windmill after missing a putt is a great way to weed out a loser), but that's precisely why it's a great married date as well. Not only do you have the chance to walk around, hold hands, flirt, and cheer each other on, it's the only sport where a girl can wear date-worthy high heels.

9. *Bookstore Browsing*—The deal is simple. You each get $10 to spend on books, magazines, or coffee. Bonus points if you can find all those "I-don't-know-what-to-get" Barnes & Noble gift cards from your coworkers at the last office Christmas party. Double-bonus points if you can agree on a book to purchase together and have enough money left over to split a grande latte in the bookstore café.

10. *Taster's Choice*—We've been to several tastings over the years—cheese tastings, coffee tastings, and even an olive oil and balsamic tasting. Use your $20 to buy your favorite that you can both agree on.

11. *Movie Swap*—It's embarrassing how many DVDs we own. They are the fallback gift our kids give to each of us.

Plus, we're so incompatible when it comes to our tastes in movies that it's just easier for us to wait for things to come out on DVD. (That way I can still get credit for watching the movie with my husband, even if I'm just "resting my eyes.") Despite our library taking up tons of living room space, there are still days when we peruse our friends' collections and think, "Ooohhhh, I'd like to see that." For those movies you'd like to watch but don't need to own, swap discs with another family. But keep a list of what's been loaned; it's better for everyone's relationship if you do.

12. *Coupon Craze*—Everyone around my house mocks me for clipping coupons—that is until we want to eat out *and* stick to our budget. Look for the buy-one-get-one-free offers in the newspaper or in the coupon junk mail. I've also gone to several restaurants' websites and signed up for their special email offers. I have a separate email account for all this requested "junk," so when I'm looking for someplace to go, I just log on to that account and look for the latest special offer.

13. *Hiking*—I hear there are people who actually enjoy this. Whatever.

14. *Going to a Farmers' Market*—OK, so this will not technically cost less than $20, but the good news is that you can use part of your grocery budget for your shopping list.

15. *Cookout*—Pack up the marshmallows and hot dogs. Find a day-camp site and let your man cook over an open fire. This used to be a hard date for me until Roger bought me a Coleman coffeemaker and a comfy chair to read in. Now I look forward to day camping.

16. *The Dog Park*—I know these are traditionally reserved for singles on the prowl, but really, there is no law that says married people can't go there. It's fun for your spouse and your pup.

17. *Xbox vs. Wii*—Take control of the game controls for a night and challenge your spouse to Rock Band. If you choose to wear earplugs, at least be inconspicuous about it.

18. *I Said Board, Not Bored*—How about a good old-fashioned game of Monopoly or Twister to spice things up with your spouse. (See Bonus Projects.)

19. *Cooking Throw-down*—Find a recipe on the Food Network and shop for the ingredients (forcing yourself to keep the cost under $20). Bring it home and have fun cooking, flirting, and eating.

20. *Sex*—Need I elaborate?

Dates I Don't Recommend if You're Trying to Stick to a $20 Budget

1. *Bowling.* How retro! How fun! How expensive. Bowling is today what yachting was in the '80s—only for those with plenty of disposable income.

2. *Window shopping.* How fun! Let's walk around and drool over all the things we can't afford.

3. *Going to the movies.* If you can tell me how two people can go to the movies and get a popcorn and a drink to share for less than $20 without sneaking in through the side door, just let me know.

4. *Bringing your children to anything.* Kids automatically triple the cost of any outing. (See exceptions above.)

5. *Doing anything with people who are not on a budget.* You'll be talked into going to a restaurant you can't afford, and then you'll have to eat canned corn and pumpkin puree for the rest of the week.

10

"But My Marriage Isn't So Hot"
Happy Habits for the Rest of Us

While my church was in the midst of going through *Happy Habits for Every Couple*, one of the women in our church wrote a very raw and honest article for our newsletter. Sandra (not her real name) is a great person who loves her husband, but she was resistant to doing the projects. She agreed to let me share her observations of participating in this program in a less than perfect marriage (the kind we all have).

> The moment I read the words "Marriage Project" I cringed. This in spite of the fact that I adore the author behind the venture. The title just got to me. Let me explain. *Marriage*: I am five years into my second marriage, the first being anything but successful, and the present being…challenging (teen stepchildren for him, a diagnosis of a bipolar spouse for me—just for starters). So the word reads like a taunting black smudge on my record. *Project*: I am able to finish a scant few of my daily responsibilities, to say nothing of a full-blown project!
>
> These are two words that are indicative of my most well-publicized failures, and when united into one gleaming headline…well, you can imagine my less than enthusiastic response.
>
> I was lovingly admonished, however, to take what I could

from the project and give it my best effort regardless of the state of my marital bliss. By the time I got to *"Happy Habits for Every Couple* Encouragement Covenant," I felt doomed. When I read the words, a spray of Diet Coke burst from my mouth. Were they serious? Could you imagine my husband and me doing anything as cute, cohesive, and healthy as signing a covenant…of any kind…together?

> Few of us have it so together that the project will be a blissful walk in a starlit park.

Further proof of inevitable failure came with each subsequent turn of the page. In dismay I tried to picture other couples not only going through *Happy Habits* together, but giggling as they filled in their project calendars.

When I had worked myself into a bitter and deluded funk—believing that all the other couples were, at that very moment, engaging in nurturing, give-and-take conversations about the spiritual state of their relationships wherein both partners were left feeling validated, respected, and united—God gently thunked me on the back of the head.

He is always good—isn't He?—to meet us where we are. Tender and sweet, in spite of ourselves. It was at this ugly point in my attitude that God reminded me of how things really are. First, few of us have it so together that *Happy Habits for Every Couple* will be a blissful walk in a starlit park; there are many fellow failures among us feeling just as inadequate or neglected who would rather not participate than spend 21 days focusing on a very sore subject. Second, in spite of what we may lack in our marriage, and regardless of how very little we resemble other couples, I already well know how exceptionally beautiful is my particular silver lining. God has always been good to fill my weird little world with His presence and joy and to remind me again of the extravagance with which my cup runneth over.

Third, apparently I was missing the point of *Happy Habits* altogether.

So I picked up the material again and read. Well-written, creative…and I wanted to be in a place where we could embrace it. But in spite of my growing support of the project, it just didn't always fit. In response I prayed, "They want him to write a list of the things he likes about me. Sounds excruciating for him. Can't I just tiptoe quietly into his reading room, tuck my head under his chin, and try not to be annoying instead?"

Then it happened. The light went on. I almost heard an audible *ding ding ding*.

My mind went into action, and the process went as follows: I don't have to worry if my spouse is less than enthused, non-present, or too exhausted to cooperate. The project is about *my* part, and it's not my job to fixate on our failures or try to solve all our problems in 21 days (shudder). *My* job, simply put, is to bless my spouse.

I suppose it should have been obvious that it was more about *my* heart attitude than trying to accomplish specific tasks. So, fellow failures, let's not throw our books away. I say we give *Happy Habits for Every Couple* another look-see and ask God what we can do to make it our own.

As for me, I will do all I can to bless my mate, regardless of the response or result. That's my marriage project.

Glossary of Terms

Project

A provided activity by which you'll bless your spouse, making him (or her) feel special and loved, while strengthening your relationship along the way! There are 21 *Projects* in all.

Major Projects

There are three *Major Projects*, one for each week. What are these? Dates. You're required to date your mate once a week. Three types of dates are suggested; you choose the nights and the times. Kids are *not* allowed on these dates; a babysitter is a Major Project must. Use the Project Planner on pages 215-18 to help you plan your Major Projects.

Bonus Projects

Sex. Yep, that's what the *Bonus Projects* are all about. Sex, plain and (not so) simple. You'll be finding ways to physically bless each other at least once a week for each of the three weeks. No doubt these projects will be some of the guys' favorites (I assume it's part of the reason so many of them are willing to participate), and I pray they'll be some of the gals' favorites as well.

Project Manager

Each of you is a *Project Manager*—this is not a one-sided proposition. It will take effort and talent from both of you to get every benefit you can from this experience.

Encouragement Crew

This is another couple who will encourage you along the way and help keep your feet to the fire. Your *Encouragement Crew* will join you in this project and collectively discuss your plans and goals and provide enthusiasm, inspiration, and maybe a little laughter along the way. We tend to stay committed to a project when we know someone is going to ask about it. You will do the same for this couple.

Project Reports

Some of the earliest *Project Managers* put *Happy Habits for Every Couple* to the test and gladly shared some of their success stories. Not only are they entertaining to read, but you can find some inspiring ideas too. *Project Reports* are highlighted at the end of each *Project*.

Getting Creative

Unique, fresh, and specific ideas...just what you need to help you complete each *Project*. Sometimes the hardest part in running the race is getting off the starting block. To help you overcome this initial inertia, each *Project* features a *Getting Creative* section to get you motivated and mobilized to bless your spouse.

Building Up Your Marriage:

Launching
Happy Habits for
Every Couple

The Send-Off

Congratulations! I am very excited that you've made a commitment to become an expert on your own marriage.

There are going to be some days when *Happy Habits for Every Couple* is hard to complete. Kids are needy, your job is stressful, and running around to find just the right special treat for your mate is going to seem overwhelming (and a little silly).

My prayer is that you don't become discouraged. Your spouse is worth it, you are worth it, and your marriage is worth it.

My prayer for you (as it is for my own marriage) is found in 2 Thessalonians 3:5: "May the Lord direct your hearts into God's love and Christ's perseverance."

God has great things in store for your marriage. Have loads of fun discovering (or rediscovering) them.

Week One Projects

Project 1

In Less Time Than a Bad Sitcom
Give Each Other 30 Minutes

*"Let the wife make the husband glad to come home,
and let him make her sorry to see him leave."*
Martin Luther

Your Project

Focus on giving each other 30 minutes of guilt-free time today. Would he like to be left alone to rest and rejuvenate? Does she want some undivided attention from you? Ask your partner what's important to him or her, and then make it happen.

Purpose of the Project
Serving One Another

This project gives you the perfect opportunity to serve each other unselfishly. Make sure you discuss the night before what will truly serve your partner, and don't assume that what ministers to you will be the same for your spouse.

A cranky old cat is one of the best things that's ever happened to my marriage.

When Roger and I got married, we each contributed two teenagers to the mix; but I came with a bonus—Zorro, the cat with attitude.

Zorro was a pound kitty that I adopted several years before Roger and I started dating. He's a white cat with a black mask (hence his name), and he has more than his share of issues. Zorro's main challenge in life is that he doesn't get along—with anyone. He barely tolerates my daughter Kimber and me (I am the keeper of the kitty kibble). Everyone else, he would just as soon see dead.

You think I'm kidding? My cat is allowed out only on even numbered days because we have to share the outdoors with a neighborhood of cats whose owners don't want them beaten to within an inch of one of their nine lives. More than once Zorro has come home from an evening on the town, and I've wondered, "Hmmm, is that his blood he's tracking in, or some other cat's?"

> Once he's had a few minutes to decompress and wind down, my husband is so much more equipped to meet my needs.

I've become the mom that I used to curse back when my kids were in school. Others are probably saying, "Doesn't she see that her kid's a bully? Why doesn't she do anything about it?" Guilty. My kid is the bad seed. I would blame it on a dysfunctional childhood, but since I adopted him as a kitten, that doesn't exactly look good for me.

It looked like Zorro was condemned to a James Dean existence—a "live fast, die young, and leave a trail of wounded kitties in your dust" kind of legacy.

That is, until I married Roger.

Roger is not a cat lover. He never envisioned himself living with anything of the feline persuasion. In fact, when he proposed, he asked if perhaps my mom (whose home I was living in during this time) would be willing to keep Zorro. While his naïveté was endearing, my mother made it clear, "You take the girl, you take the cat."

So Roger and Zorro became roommates by default, and neither of their lives has been the same since.

You see, Zorro is in love with Roger. *In love* with him, I tell you. Sitting-by-the-front-door-can't-wait-for-him-to-get-home in love with him.

My cat's favorite part of every day is when Roger comes through that front door, and that is when Zorro starts barking at Roger. Cats don't bark, you say? Trust me, this one does. Zorro's whole goal is to get Roger upstairs and lying down on our bed so they can catch a 15-minute nap together.

It really is a little weird.

But what Zorro figured out long before I did was that Roger needs that quick lie-down to transition from work to home. While I know my husband could do without the cat in his "catnap," that crazy kitty helped us discover a great transitional routine that leads to a relaxed Roger.

But woe to me if Roger doesn't get to lie down. He braves on, getting through the evening, but I can tell the persistent thought running through his head at dinner is, *Wow, those mashed potatoes look like they'd make a comfortable pillow.*

So I do my best to protect Roger and his 15-30 minutes. It doesn't work out every night, but whenever possible, I make it a priority for him to transition.

And he does the same for me. While my time doesn't involve snuggling with a cat, I usually need *something* from Roger—going over our schedule for the evening, barbecuing the chicken, figuring out why the printer *still* won't print, or disciplining any wayward kids that need to be brought back in line.

Once he's had a few minutes to decompress and wind down, my husband is so much more equipped to meet my needs.

But I'm Tired Too

I feel like I'm treading on dangerous ground here.

In most homes (including ours upon occasion), I know it's a tense standoff where everyone is working hard and all the adults are tired at the end of a very long day.

If you've been at home all day with kids who have little concern for your emotional well being, who don't look at you with compassion in their eyes and say, "Hey Mom, why don't you go lie down for a few minutes? I can change my own diaper," your first instinct may be to throw said children at their other parent as soon as he walks through the front door. I get it—I've done my fair share of baby tossing in my life.

On the other hand, if you've had a long, stress-filled day at work, all you may want to do is come home and hide from those kids.

> "For by the grace given me I say to every one of you: Do not think of yourself more highly than you ought, but rather think of yourself with sober judgment, in accordance with the faith God has distributed to each of you" (Romans 12:3).

This is where it's critical to put our spouse's needs above our own. It's imperative to not just focus on how stressful our day has been, but to imagine what our partner has gone through in his or her day.

So, if you're the one home all day, you may just want to play the "Daddy isn't really home yet" game for another half hour, or say to your wife, "I'm taking the kids to the park," or "You take the first half hour to chill, and I'll take the second." Do your best to resist those urges to unload your frustrations, and your kids, during your spouse's gift of downtime.

Or if you are the one getting home after a long day, it may be critical to pitch in as soon as you get through the door, and then transition a bit later. Each family and couple is different.

No Family Games Night Tonight

Have you ever been in a conversation with a one-upman? You know the type. It doesn't matter how bad your day was, this person's day was just a little bit worse.

It doesn't matter the great thing your kid did in school today, her kid is just a little bit better.

If you stubbed your toe, he broke his.

If your husband barbecued, her husband went out and slaughtered the cow.

Doesn't matter if your situation is good or bad, exciting or exhausting, the one-upman is, in the words of my favorite Dana Carvey character, the Church Lady, "Just a little bit superior."

Let's leave the martyr at the door.

That's one of the benefits of being married—having a soft place to land at the end of a long day. But in order for that to happen, I must to be willing to lay down some of my rights and expectations so I can *be* that soft place for my spouse.

We need to recognize that whatever role God has called us to, our spouse has a role as well—just as important, just as needed in the body of Christ. And at the end of the day, much is required from each of us.

The surest way to bring peace to everyone in the household is to give just a little by putting the other person's needs in front of our own.

Prayer for Today

God, help me to release my expectations for _____ (my spouse) and focus on how I can bless him or her today.

Getting Creative

- Ask your spouse what he needs. Does your husband want to go hide in the garage for 30 minutes? Does your wife want you to take the baby so she can shower by herself? Asking what your partner needs will avoid the counterproductive situation that comes from assuming that what is restful and rejuvenating to you is the same thing your spouse is dreaming of.

- Are you home with the kids when your mate gets home? If it won't interrupt nap or dinner routines, what about taking the kids with you as you run some errands at the end of the day to give your spouse some quiet time when he or she gets off the job? Errands that don't require kids to get out of the car include: filling the gas tank, banking at the drive-thru ATM, picking up dinner at curbside takeout, using the drive-thru window at the pharmacy, returning your library books at the drive-thru drop off.

- Sometimes quiet is not what your love is hoping for. Maybe your spouse wants some uninterrupted time, just with you. Be sure to ask.

- Don't be offended if your mate does enjoy a little quiet reprieve; it's not about getting away from you. Promise.

Project Reports

"I let Terrin sleep in and kept the house quiet by taking our daughter Rachel to her class. Later, he let me read on the porch for 30 minutes and took our other daughter, Rebecca, to the appliance store (not the place I like to go!) to check out refrigerators and microwaves. It was great for me to not have to go, and he enjoyed the extra sleep."—Sherry

"The NBA Finals was on, and I sacrificed watching the game to spend time with my wife at her favorite store even though I really wanted to watch the game. Although we both like sports, this project encouraged me to spend quality time with my wife doing what she wanted to do."—Harlenn

Your Plan for the Project *(copy your plan on the Project Planner at the back of this book)*

Results *(mate's reaction, my reaction)*

Project 2

It's All About Her
Make Her a Hallmark Holiday

*"There must be millions of people all over the world who
never get any love letters...I could be their leader."*

CHARLIE BROWN

Your Project

Husbands, you guessed it. You have to go into a store, look
through the cards, find one that declares your love for your
wife (or talks about a private joke you two share), purchase
the overpriced card, write just one sentence in it, sign your
name, and put it somewhere creative where she will find it.
(No cards containing jokes about age or weight are allowed.)

Purpose of the Project
Encouragement

We all need to know that we're appreciated. Guys, you get to be
your wife's main encouragement today.

A confession for all you wives out there: Oh, how I hated the
Proverbs 31 woman. If you're new to the Bible, let me give you a
glimpse of her:

- She's the woman who always looks like the "After" in the
"Before and After" pictures in *InStyle* magazine.

- She is the annoying mom on your kid's soccer team who makes homemade organic snacks, and all the kids actually eat them.
- She works morning until night without a power nap.
- All of her family's meals are grown locally and made at home. The "perfect" wife would never even consider takeout.
- She's an entrepreneur, a homemaker, and a dutiful wife. Put another way, "she can bring home the bacon, fry it up in a pan, and never ever let him forget he's a man" (you must be over 40 to get this reference).
- Oh, and her children are perfect.

I have to tell you, she was giving me a complex.

I admit that I have gone through phases of trying to be the best wife I possibly can. I have worked and raised kids and done all the right stuff—and was absolutely miserable. I was trying to live out some unobtainable version of what I thought being the "good wife" looked like. I would look at the best of the women around me, the Proverbs 31 women, and feel totally inadequate all the time. I got to the point where I just gave up—if I couldn't be perfect, why try at all. It never occurred to me that God created me the way that He did because He liked me. I just figured that God was constantly disappointed with me in every regard.

> Husbands, your encouragement can go a long way in giving us confidence to say yes to what God has called us to be.

Recently, I actually tried to sit down and study Proverbs 31. The first line blew me away: "Who can find a virtuous and capable wife?" (v. 10 NLT). I love that! The fact that being a virtuous wife is difficult is laid out there for us. This "wife stuff" is really, really hard. It's hard to be everything that everyone wants (or needs) us to be. Being a great and honorable wife takes a lot of different skills. And it takes a lot of effort.

Husbands, your encouragement can go a long way in giving us confidence to say no to an unobtainable notion of what a wife should be and to say yes to what God has called us to be. When we as wives know that our actions cause you to feel loved and respected, suddenly failing to spin our own fabrics isn't so guilt inducing.

We can't rely on our own strength as wives or as husbands. We need guidance and the power of God every step of the way—not only to give us strength to finish the things we're supposed to do but also to sustain us as we say *no* to those things we're not supposed to do.

The best marriages are the ones where each partner is regularly thinking, "How can I let _____ know that I appreciate him?" As a spouse, I may not always be the person my partner wants me to be, but I'm always doing something that can be praised and appreciated.

> "And let us consider how we may spur one another on toward love and good deeds" (Hebrews 10:24).

"People have a way of becoming what you encourage them to be, not what you nag them to be."—Anonymous

Prayer for Today

Dear God, help me say *yes* to everything You want for me and my marriage, and *no* to those things that are not part of Your plan for my life. Help me to also be an encouragement to my partner, every day.

Getting Creative

Places you could leave a card for her to find:

- On the seat of the car
- On the wall of the garage (so when she pulls in she'll see it)
- Inside her coffee travel mug before the coffee goes in (make sure it's highly visible)
- Mailed to her office (making sure the note is G-rated)

- Inside her favorite magazine you know she'll read today
- Taped to the bathroom mirror
- At your local coffee shop (see if the barista will deliver the card with your sweetie's regular drive-thru order; leave a big tip)
- Inside the box of microwave popcorn she'll snack on tonight
- On the DVR remote
- In the mailbox (finally, something besides credit card applications)

Project Reports

"My husband bought me a blank card with a puppy on the front. We've been together for over 23 years, and in the card he told me something he has never told me before. This probably was one of the most meaningful projects to me because he normally doesn't write anything but his name in a card and never buys one for me just because. After being together so long, it meant a lot to me to find out something new."—Rachael

"I went to Walgreens at lunch. Decided on the more serious card rather than the funny card I would normally get. I didn't hide it, just gave it to her directly. I wrote about how important she is to me, and how much fun it is to watch her grow into a godly woman."—Elliot

"We were on vacation when this project came up, so I figured he would just skip it. Instead, I crawled into bed and found the card on my pillow. I think of my husband as being pretty thoughtful all the time, but I could tell that he took a lot of thought and time in writing this card and telling me what I meant to him. It's the best card I've ever received from him. It made me feel very loved."—Marie

Here's an idea from my husband: one Valentine's Day he cut up almost 100 cards with cute words and sayings and put them in a decorated box for me to open and look through. Trust me, that box will be saved and looked at for the rest of my life.

Your Plan for the Project *(copy your plan on the Project Planner at the back of this book)*

Results *(mate's reaction, my reaction)*

Getting to Know You
Get the Vital Stats on Your Mate

*"Oh, the comfort, the inexpressible comfort of feeling
safe with a person, having neither to weigh thoughts nor
measure words, but pouring them all out, just as they
are, chaff and grain together, certain that a faithful hand
will take and sift them, keep what is worth keeping,
and with a breath of kindness blow the rest away."*
GEORGE ELIOT

Your Project

Each of you fill out the survey below so the next time you
want to bless your spouse, you have all the information you
need. Your gift will be right on target, making it even more
appreciated.

Purpose of the Project

Even if your spouse *should* know the answers to these questions,
please put something down for each category. The more thorough
you are, the more confident your partner will be when it comes to
blessing you.

Date of birth:

Date of anniversary:

Other date(s) he or she needs to know (and why):

Favorite foods:

Favorite restaurants:

Favorite dinner:

Favorite flowers:

Favorite perfume/cologne:

Favorite music artists:

Favorite authors or magazines:

Favorite clothing store:

Your clothing and shoe sizes:

Favorite Starbucks order:

Suggestions of a treat he or she could buy:

I want you each to fill out the survey for a couple of reasons:

1. You can shop with confidence, knowing that the little treat you pick up for your sweetie will be something they love, and that they don't have to fake delight when you buy them the wrong dark chocolate.
2. So the following marriage testing conversation doesn't happen to you.

"And when is your birthday?" the salesclerk at Bare Escentuals asked me while ringing up my makeup. (Yikes! Since when does it take over $300 of products for me to obtain the natural look?)

I was busy looking through my bag of goodies when Roger answered for me. "Her birthday is April—"

I immediately looked up from my eyeliner. "Um, honey...my birthday is in June. April would be your first wife's."

Gulp.

For some couples that little exchange would have led to hours of silent sulking and punishing looks and behavior. And at the beginning of our marriage, I would have behaved exactly that way or worse.

Now don't get me wrong. I can still hold a grudge over minor infractions with the best of them. (Just let someone in our house forget to put the cans on the curb on garbage night. Go ahead, I dare you.) But I have learned after many miserable days that my holding infractions over Roger's head not only makes him miserable, but it also makes me an ugly person to be around. (Regardless of how much makeup I just bought.)

> Holding infractions over my husband's head not only makes him miserable, but it also makes me an ugly person to be around.

Oh, and just a little tip for all of you who have a hard time remembering birthdays and anniversaries. This past April, Roger took me out for my un-birthday. I enjoyed an entire evening of my husband's undivided attention, along with dinner out, a chick flick, and a brand-new outfit.

I hope he messes up our anniversary too.

What Jesus Says about Grudges

The words of Jesus show only too strongly how He felt about those who hold grudges: "For if you forgive other people when they sin against you, your heavenly Father will also forgive you. But if you do not forgive others their sins, your Father will not forgive your sins" (Matthew 6:14-15).

While grace goes against our nature, it's vital to the growth of our marriages and our own relationship with Christ. There is no room for grudges.

Prayer for Today

Dear God, let me not be a grudge-holder. Grow my heart to be more like Yours so that my first impulse is always grace.

Getting Creative

Once you are in possession of the information from the survey, be sure to do the following:

- Put it somewhere safe—in your smartphone or in your sock drawer; wherever you will be able to retrieve it when you need it.

- Put important dates on your calendar. Better yet, note it a few days before the actual date so that you'll have time to do what needs to be done.

Project Reports

"We really liked the survey. It definitely gave us some ideas. We will be using the ideas in the near future."—Sabrina

"The survey was a little help but…no brags, just facts. I'm pretty good with gifts and her size etc. I knew most of the answers without having to ask her. But it is nice to have it all in one place."—Elliot

Your Plan for the Project *(copy your plan on the Project Planner at the back of this book)*

Results *(mate's reaction, my reaction)*

Project 4

Sweet Treat

Doing Something Special Just for Him

*"It is one of the most beautiful compensations of life,
that no man can sincerely try to help
another without helping himself."*

RALPH WALDO EMERSON

Your Project

Wives: Make, bake, or purchase your guy's favorite treat. It can be a dessert just for him, his favorite cut of steak, or a gift certificate to his favorite restaurant. While doing that, make sure it's *his* favorite and not yours, and let him know that it's perfectly OK not to share with you, the kids, or the dog.

Purpose of the Project

That's right, ladies, I'm asking you to serve your husband today. OK, now let's all take a deep breath.

For some of you, the whole "servant thing" isn't a big deal, but for some of us (myself included) being a servant is what the ladies on *The View* would call a "Hot Topic."

You have to understand that my formative years—the '70s—were spent with a working mother in a society that still didn't quite know what it thought about that. My mom was also part of a union, so my little brother, Brian, and I walked a couple of picket lines in our day. Much of that effort was based (rightly, in my opinion) on getting fair treatment and a fair wage. However, if I carry those attitudes into other areas of my life, being unwilling to lay down some "rights" and serve others—including my spouse (whether I am a wife or a husband)—I'm missing one of the biggest blessings I can receive from being married.

True joy comes from learning to be a servant and serving our spouses, families, and others—whether it's bringing home a paycheck, making a comfortable home, caring for family members, or some combination of all the above.

Choosing to Be a Servant

I love Richard Foster's explanation in his book *Celebration of Discipline: The Path to Spiritual Growth* about what it means to choose to be a servant:

> A natural and understandable hesitancy accompanies any serious discussion of service. The hesitancy is prudent since it is wise to count the cost before plunging headlong into any Discipline. We experience a fear that comes out something like this: "If I do that, people will take advantage of me; they will walk all over me." Right here we must see the difference between choosing to serve and choosing to be a servant. When we choose to serve, we are still in charge. We decide whom we will serve and when we will serve. And if we are in charge, we will worry a great deal about anyone stepping on us, that is, taking charge over us.

> "When we choose to be a servant, we give up the right to be in charge."

> But when we choose to be a servant, we give up the right to be in charge. There is great freedom in this. If we voluntarily choose to be taken advantage of, then we cannot be manipulated. When we choose to be a servant, we surrender

the right to decide when we will serve. We become available and vulnerable.

I love what Foster says here about all the power (or lack thereof) that lies in our choice to be a servant. When we make that choice, no one can take advantage of us because the decision to serve is ours.

Prayer for Today

Dear God, let my thoughts be on how to serve _____ (my mate). May he have peace knowing that he has my heart.

Getting Creative

- Make brownies for him. There's nothing that makes my husband happier than the aroma of brownies baking in the oven when he gets home. Hint: for this project you'll need to make two batches if you have kids at home.
- Is your husband more of a steak guy than a sweet-tooth guy? A gift certificate to Outback Steakhouse may be just the thing to make his night.
- If you won't see your husband all day, how about leaving a Starbucks card in his car for him to pick up a treat?

Project Reports

"So, the project today was really fun and easy. I was challenged to surprise my husband with a yummy treat for his tummy! I made two: (1) Yummy homemade triple chocolaty brownies, warm from the oven and neatly arranged on a pretty plate when he arrived home, and (2) a very interesting jambalaya, all simmered together to create a wonderful flavorful dinner. I really enjoyed surprising him with this tonight. I even cleared off the table and put on the pretty tablecloth my mom gave me a few years ago. Overall, the dinner and brownies were really enjoyed, and my hubby went to bed with an overly stuffed tummy!"—Wendy

"A treat just for him—Cheetos. OK, over the past few years my husband has lost about 50 pounds. Prior to losing that weight, he really loved to eat Cheetos in bed. He has since replaced the Cheetos and now eats almonds in bed. I thought it would be a nice treat for him to have his Cheetos just this once. I have to say he was very surprised when I gave them to him. (Big smile on his face as if to say, 'Ahhhh, the memories!')"—Penny

Your Plan for the Project *(copy your plan on the Project Planner at the back of this book)*

Results *(mate's reaction, my reaction)*

Project 5

Turning Up the Heat
Cooking Together

*"A major reason capable people fail to advance is
that they don't work well with their colleagues."*
LEE IACOCCA

Your Project

Simply cook a meal together. This can be just for the two of
you, your family, or invite some guests over. You can either
cook the whole meal together or each of you can cook items
separately.

Purpose of the Project

Relationships are built on trust. Trust is built on experience. Experience is best built by teamwork.

I never feel like more of a team with my husband than when
company's comin'.

For the most part, Roger and I do our own thing during the day
and most evenings too. He goes off to work each day; I stay at home
and write or I'm on the road traveling. After dinner, many of our
evenings are dedicated to our individual ministries, our individual
kids (being a blended family), or *Project Runway*. But when we have
friends over, everything changes.

Of course, there's the mad dash-and-stash that happens before
anyone who's not blood related crosses our front door. (Oh please,

don't tell me that your house is always picked up all the time. And if it is, I don't think we can be friends.) But my favorite part of entertaining is cooking with my hubby. After 10 years, we have some firmly established roles when it comes to entertaining.

Me:

> Figure out the menu
> Shop for what we need
> Make the appetizer
> Make the salad
> Make the dessert

Him:

> *Grunt.* Cook meat on fire. *Grunt.*

OK, I'm oversimplifying a bit.

Roger really does pitch in to make everything happen, but I know his favorite part is getting the steaks to come out just so. Also, there's a method to our madness when it comes to the division of our entertaining roles. I would much rather get everything on my list done before people arrive so I can sit and chat with our guests, whereas Roger is much better off staying busy (read: *out of sight*) as people arrive, leaving the hosting duties to me, his way-more outgoing wife.

> One of the reasons we love cooking together is that we both get to explore our strengths.

I used to feel guilty that he was slaving over a hot Weber while I was sitting back with my iced Diet Coke, chatting with our guests. But after several years of marriage, I've figured out this works for us.

Roger and I work together on a lot of projects, but one of the reasons we love cooking together is that we both get to explore our strengths. I can praise him extravagantly for how great his tri-tip comes out, and he's never at a loss for a compliment when it comes to my artichoke dip.

One Couple-ing

"For this reason a man will leave his father and mother and be united to his wife, and the two will become one flesh. This is a profound mystery" (Ephesians 5:31).

Authors Debra White Smith and Daniel W. Smith talk about this teamwork concept in their book, *Romancing Your Wife,* and give some examples of what a marriage looks like when two people live out Ephesians 5:31, becoming what they call "One Couple." One Couples...

- think in terms of "we and us," not "me and you" or "my and mine"
- are free to be themselves and exercise all their gifts
- have marriages that are love-based, not rule- or control-based
- don't care which spouse earns the most. Love and respect thrive based on the essence of who the spouse is, not what the spouse earns.
- do everything possible to empower each other. One spouse never looks at the other and says, "Your role is to empower me" or "You're supposed to pour yourself into me while I pursue my interests."
- aren't threatened by each other's gifts and talent, but freely applaud each other's accomplishments
- are best friends
- argue infrequently because they are of one mind

Prayer for Today

Dear God, we want to be a "One Couple," building each other up and serving each other in every way.

Getting Creative

- Not a cook? See if you can learn how to make your mate's favorite food. Ask your husband to give you a lesson on the barbecue or ask your wife how the bread machine works. It's not cheating if your spouse helps you in the kitchen. (Just make sure that you clean up your own mess.)

- This doesn't have to be a surprise. In fact, it will be more fun if you plan it together.

- Don't worry if his favorite is Thai noodles and hers is pancakes. Being eclectic is half the fun.

Project Reports

"Cooking together was cool. It's just nice to have that time dedicated to work together on something and get to talk or manage the kids together rather than one of us cooking and the other watching the kids."—Lee

Your Plan for the Project *(copy your plan on the Project Planner at the back of this book)*

Results *(mate's reaction, my reaction)*

Project 6

Burning Passion and Burning Calories

Getting Active Together

"Remember this: your body is your slave; it works for you."
JACK LALANNE

Your Project

Turn off the TV and take some time to connect through exercise.

Purpose of the Project

Not only are you working toward healthier bodies, but also toward a healthier marriage. Make sure that you are cheering each other on as you push to go that extra mile (both literally and figuratively).

We have a friend couple who go running together every day. (A "friend couple" is any couple where we are friends with both the husband and wife, not just us wives being friends and dragging the husbands along to couples' bocce ball.)

One of the reasons Jim and Marta have such a great marriage is that they exercise together. It's only a couple of times a week, but in those times they're reaching for mutual goals (finishing without passing out), cheering each other on, and have something to talk endlessly about over dinner (mainly running shoes and marathons, I would imagine). Hmmm, come to think of it, I'm not really sure why we are friends.

But the biggest benefit is that as they are spending time together. They are staying connected, not missing the ups and downs of their partner.

Missed Signals

I'm kind of oblivious when it comes to cars. I know people (mainly guys, but a few chicks as well) who can wax poetic about carburetors and horsepower all day long. Some people just grow up in car families where Saturdays are spent under the hood, and their DVRs are filled with reruns of *American Chopper.*

Me? I'm annoyed when I have to decide between different grades of gas.

So when as a 16-year-old I passed my driver's test (barely—don't let anyone tell you that a healthy amount of flirting won't get you anywhere at the DMV), it was time to start looking for my own set of wheels.

After absolute minutes of searching, I found my dream (i.e., cheap) car—a bright orange '74 Honda.

Now this was a very special car. I bet all you car guys are wondering if this fine piece of machinery was an automatic or stick (see, I do know some insider jargon). Oh no, it was much more special than that. It was a *Hondamatic.* It had three gears, and when it sounded as though the hamsters were running really fast, that was the time to shift.

So, with my deep love of all things automotive, it really should come as no shock that when it came to taking care of my first car, I could always find better things to do with my time and money (why bother with tiresome things like oil changes when Nordstrom was having its semiannual shoe sale?).

Everything with my Honda was going great until about three months into owning it. That's when the little red warning light popped on.

I knew enough about cars to realize that the red warning light meant something bad (read: *expensive*) was going on inside the car. I didn't have a lot of extra money at the time (remember the shoes), so I figured my best course of action was to ignore it.

And that worked for a couple of weeks. But every time I got into the car, that light just *bugged* me. It was such an annoyance that I knew it was time to take action. So I took duct tape (every handyman's friend, right?) and placed a square piece over the warning light. And for four months, the duct tape and I had the situation under control. The car kept going, and I didn't feel guilty about not dealing with the problem.

That is until the engine caught fire.

Yep, just a big ball of flames, barreling down the street. And that's when I realized that maybe, just maybe, that warning light was something I should have paid a little more attention to.

Staying Connected

I am easily distracted by so many things in life it's easy to miss (and foolish to ignore) those little "warning lights"—especially in my marriage. That's why staying connected is so vital to the health and longevity of my relationship.

My husband and I both have busy schedules (because we're adults living in the twenty-first century, I realize that statement is a given), and it would be oh so easy to cruise along for weeks without really connecting or even realizing it, either. We need to be absolutely intentional about creating times to connect.

"If you have any encouragement from being united with Christ, if any comfort from his love, if any common sharing in the Spirit, if any tenderness and compassion, then make my joy complete by being like-minded, having the same love, being one in spirit and of one mind" (Philippians 2:1-2).

Not only do we need to be watching for those warning lights in our marriage (longer hours at work, less dating and more fighting, sharpness in our tone, less of a desire to put our spouse before us), but we need to make sure that we are physically spending time together so that we can prevent those problems from arising.

Some of the ways that work for many couples are:

- Evening walks around their neighborhood
- Eating dinner together whenever they are both in town
- Eating lunch together at least twice a week
- Praying on the phone together when they are apart
- Going to bed at the same time
- Weekly date nights

Now some of these things may not work for you. I get it, and I'm sure you have ways of connecting that wouldn't work for us or our friends. But if you're waiting for some time to magically open up, there are going to be a lot of missed warning lights along the way.

Prayer for Today

God, when You call me to, help me to make that extra effort in whatever area of my marriage that I need to.

Getting Creative

An evening walk counts if that's all you have the time (or energy) for.

If you're into extreme sports (anything where you hang by a rope or jump off bridges), make sure to take your spouse's comfort and "fear factor" into consideration.

The purpose of this project is to get you to spend some time connecting with each other. So make sure whatever form of exercise you choose doesn't leave you so winded that you can't talk while you're doing it.

Also, no iPods while doing this activity together. It's so much easier to connect when no technology gets in the way.

Project Reports

"Scott and I actually work out together using the P90X fitness program. It isn't very romantic, but it is good spending time together and making fun of the way I can't do even half of it!"—Kelli

"We walk together daily, at least once and usually twice a day. It's a great way to stay connected as it's just the two of us (well, and the dog)."—Sherry

"I wasn't really interested in going to the gym, and we can't talk if he's on the stationary bike and I'm on the treadmill, so we went for a nice walk in our neighborhood."—Penny

Your Plan for the Project *(copy your plan on the Project Planner at the back of this book)*

Make sure whatever form of exercise you choose doesn't leave you so winded that you can't talk while you're doing it.

Results *(mate's reaction, my reaction)*

Project 7

A Day to Pray
Present Your Spouse's Requests to God

*"We must alter our lives in order to alter our hearts,
for it is impossible to live one way and pray another."*
WILLIAM LAW

Your Project

Ask your spouse what he or she would like prayer for, write it down, and then remember to pray throughout your day for the requests your partner has given you.

Purpose of the Project
Planning for a Great Marriage

The biggest thing we can do in planning for a great marriage is to pray for that marriage. Most positive actions that we make happen in our marriage are the result of prayer.

Some people may criticize this book because the projects don't feel spiritual enough. If this book really is about the foundations of a Christian marriage, shouldn't it have a lot more prayer and Bible verses?

Now I believe you must pray for and with your spouse regularly—if it were not for prayer, I wonder how long Roger and I would have stayed married—but most of us need to move to action in our marriages as well as to pray. And *Happy Habits for Every Couple* is about *action!*

As James warns the readers of his New Testament letter:

> Do not merely listen to the word, and so deceive yourselves. Do what it says. Anyone who listens to the word but does not do what it says is like someone who looks at his face in a mirror and, after looking at himself, goes away and immediately forgets what he looks like. But whoever looks intently into the perfect law that gives freedom, and continues in it—not forgetting what they have heard, but doing it—they will be blessed in what they do (James 1:22-25).

How to Pray for Your Marriage

I wish I were one of those people who springs out of bed in the morning eager to sit at God's feet and read His Word. But He and I are usually not on talking terms until the second cup of coffee.

> Prayer has not been natural or come easily to me. I need help. The good news is that I am not alone.

It has taken me a couple of decades to be OK with that. I have always felt like a less-than Christian because prayer has not been natural or come easily to me. I need help.

The good news is that I am not alone. If I were, then the market wouldn't be flooded with books on how to pray for the person we love. Stormie Omartian's *The Power of a Praying*...series has sold more than 11 million copies, so let's just assume that corner of the market is adequately covered, shall we?

But there are just times I need the idiot's guide. I need to be reminded that my guy needs encouragement at the end of a hard day. I need to be reminded that it is not always about me and a "what have you done for me lately?" attitude. There are times I need to be reminded to say "I love you" even when neither of us is being very lovable.

None of this detracts from the need to pray and go into God's Word. But at the end of the day, we need to make sure that we are not just praying about how to live, or reading about how to live, but that we are also practicing how to live.

Prayer for Today

Dear God, constantly bring my spouse to mind today and remind me to pray for him (or her), so he will know he is covered throughout the day.

Getting Creative

- Ask your spouse early in the day or even the night before so you'll know specifically how you should pray.
- Set an alarm on your cell phone to remind you to stop and pray throughout the day.
- If you know you'll spend a big part of your day either at your desk or in the car, put up a sticky note to remind you of your partner's requests.
- Send your honey a text message or email, letting her know you are praying for her.
- Be sure to ask about your spouse's day. Prayer really makes a difference!

Project Reports

"I didn't really need to ask; I already know the hot spots."
—Sherry

Your Plan for the Project *(copy your plan on the Project Planner at the back of this book)*

Results *(mate's reaction, my reaction)*

Date Your Mate
Half and Half

"Whenever I want a really nice meal, I start dating again."
SUSAN HEALY

Your Project

You both are responsible for planning your date night. Either the husband picks out the place for dinner and the wife figures out the activity, or the other way around.

Purpose of the Project

The catch? Pick the place your mate would most enjoy. It's your job to go more than halfway in serving your spouse on your special night out.

It has been a long hard week. Friday night rolls around, and I want some action. I want to go to a movie, go out to dinner, anything just to have a little fun.

The only problem? The person I'm going out with is my husband.

Now, you have to understand, I love my husband. I love spending time with him. But let's just say that his choice of entertainment leaves something to be desired.

Going to the movies is great in theory, but

> It's your job to go more than halfway in serving your spouse on your special night out.

actually having to pick one? It's easier for us to decide who's getting what in our wills than how we're going to spend two hours and the equivalent of a car payment (when you throw in a large popcorn and a couple of Diet Cokes) on our trip to the movies.

And don't even get me started on eating out. When I'm being good on my diet, I have a hard time coming up with someplace to eat. If the restaurant doesn't have a bottomless basket of chips, Roger would rather skip it.

This has led to some marital tensions.

I know it's a sacrifice for Roger to spend his hard-earned money on "chick food" at the local salad bar, just as it's a sacrifice for me to sit for two hours watching a movie with no plot line and where everything blows up at the end. (But somehow they can magically have a sequel.)

The funny thing is, once I get to that movie where everything goes *boom* or the Mexican restaurant where the main food groups are flour and oil, I end up having a pretty good time. Just being with Roger makes the whole experience more fun (and it is nice every once in a while to go to a movie without subtitles or a plot so I don't have to think).

Prayer for Today

Dear God, help us to look forward to our date together as much as or more than we looked forward to our dates before we were married.

Getting Creative

- During the days before the date, listen carefully to your spouse. Is there a new restaurant he's dying to try? Did she just start a new diet, so the new pasta place would be more of a challenge than a blessing? Keep your ears open and take note if you have to.

- Go wild. Maybe a movie is too safe. How about go-cart racing or pottery painting? Remember, it's all about pleasing the love of your life, so don't be as concerned about what you want as what will shock your sweetie (in a good way).

Your Plan for the Project *(copy your plan on the Project Planner at the back of this book)*

Results *(mate's reaction, my reaction)*

Sex

Circle It in Red on the Calendar

*"A true man does not need to romance a
different girl every night, a true man romances
the same girl for the rest of her life."*

ANA ALAS

Your Bonus Project

Keep it simple this week. Plan in advance when you will
make time for sex this week, and then do it.

Yesterday I was at a book discussion group for my first book, *The
Husband Project.* This group of about 20 women was taking the challenge together to bless their men for 21 days. I was impressed that to
kick off The Project, they committed to go
home and have sex with their husbands within
the next 48 hours.

Now that is diving into the project.

Of course the men were thrilled. But what
I found fascinating was the reaction from the
women.

One woman, Carolyn, I think said it best:
"When I planned for sex, instead of looking
at it as an interruption to my already over-
crowded life, I found that I not only enjoyed
it, but actually looked forward to it."

> Put it on
> the calendar
> and have
> something to
> look forward to,
> together.

So this week, put it on the calendar and have something to look forward to, together.

Prayer for Today

Dear God, help us make each other the priority in our lives.

Your Plan for the Project *(copy your plan on the Project Planner at the back of this book)*

Results *(mate's reaction, my reaction)*

Week Two Projects

Project 8

A Little Hands-On Attention
Give Each Other a Massage

Ross: *Phebes, why would you want to operate a drill press?*
Phoebe: *Just for some short-term work. You know,*
until I get back some of my massage clients.
Chandler: *Pirates again?*
Phoebe: *No, nothing like that. I was just such*
a dummy. I taught this "massage-yourself-
at-home workshop," and they are.
Friends

Your Project

Both of you get 15 minutes of soothing hands-on attention.
Ask your partner what kind of massage she would like (hand,
foot, back, neck), and then give it to her. You may want to
prepare a day in advance and get massage lotion. Lastly, this
is massage without benefits—so let's keep it PG-13.

Purpose of the Project
Connecting and Serving

When you serve your spouse by giving her a massage, with no
expectations or ulterior motives, you get to know things about your
partner that no one else knows. Plus, when you determine what kind
of massage your spouse likes best, you may just discover a new way
to minister to your husband or wife when life is at its most insane.

Even without leading to sex, massage is a very intimate exchange. It's important both partners have the freedom to be honest and open about what is tender and relaxing and, maybe, what is just annoying.

In order to reach that depth of connection, we need to feel secure with our spouse, knowing that whatever is shared is safe. There is no criticism or judgment, just a willingness to understand and be understood.

It takes a level of trust and commitment to be able to have those conversations with your partner, especially if physical touch is a challenge in your relationship. If that's the case, let me encourage you to begin by praying about your time together. Commit your time to God, knowing that each of you, and God, will be honored as you weave a tighter connection.

OK, I admit it. I'm a total pansy. I'm not a fan of most massages—they hurt and I try to avoid pain in most areas of my life. I don't want someone pounding on my back or contorting my legs to crack my back. Those massage chairs you sit in while getting a pedicure? My highest setting is on "Lightly Tapping." I don't even like having my hair shampooed by anyone except my own stylist because he knows I'm a sensitive girl and don't take to having my neck wrung while he's rinsing out my dye (I mean "subtle highlights").

So when I married someone whose chief love language is physical touch, I have to admit, I was hesitant to climb on the massage bandwagon.

Plenty of marriages have one partner who's totally into massage and one who's not. Roger and I have learned to meet in the middle. We found a few things that have made a big difference for us in this area. In time, you'll most likely come up with your own tool kit, but if you're new to the massage game, let me suggest:

1. *Complete Massage: A Visual Guide to Over 100 Techniques* by Clare Maxwell-Hudson

I first mentioned this fabulous book in *The Husband Project* and still have not found a better one on the subject. While the pictures in most massage books make me feel as though I'm looking at a cross between the *Sports Illustrated* Swimsuit Issue and last week's Victoria's Secret catalog, *Complete Massage* gives you all the pictures without the worry that your teenage son may come across the book. Not only does it have great photos that illustrate exactly what to do, there are also step-by-step instructions for each type of massage that interests you. It's a useful guide for the massage novice or expert.

> Learning to give a massage in order to simply connect and relax, with no expectations, is an important skill.

2. The Salad Kit

When Roger and I were first married, we spent a small fortune at our local bath and body shop. (While I may not have been a fan of massage, who can pass up a lime-scented massage lotion?) As our collection of oils and lotions grew, we realized that many of the names—Mango Oil, Almond Paste, Lemon Rub—sounded a lot like our favorite salad ingredients. So when we go away on vacation, we make sure to pack "The Salad Kit," our now not-so-undercover code name for our massage kit.

3. iPod

Have a playlist of relaxing music. It can be classical or slow jazz, anything you like. You might even try a soundtrack of nature's elements (the sound of falling rain accompanied by music). Roger and I have also swapped massages over worship music.

Warning: Bonus Project May Not Be Initiated Within 30 Minutes of This Project.

One of this project's objectives is to concentrate on nonsexual massage. To help you achieve this, it's important to talk specifically about what kind of touch is most relaxing for each of you to receive.

After interviewing several couples, I realized that men and women have two different goals from massage. (I'm speaking in generalities here, but after talking with so many people, it's easy to see a pattern emerge.) Women want a massage to relax. Men want a massage to lead to sex, and then they will relax.

Sex is important. That's why we have three Bonus Projects in this book. But learning to give a massage in order to simply connect and relax, with no expectations, is an important skill as well.

So what will your partner find soothing? This is the time *not* to make assumptions. If you ask me, there's nothing more relaxing than a foot rub with coconut-scented lotion. Roger would rather watch a half dozen Kate Hudson chick flicks than have someone touch his feet. Be bold, ask what your spouse wants, and then make it happen.

"But I Don't Wanna," and Why Jesus Said Do It Anyway

While massage is not an easy gift for some to give, we're all going to have projects that require us to stretch to bless our spouses. I've tried to make every project user-friendly, but I have to admit the massage project is one that would have me asking for a hall pass.

And that's exactly why it's so important that I don't skip it.

> If we do only the projects that make it easy for us to give, we're missing the whole point .

If we do only the projects that make it easy for us to give, we're missing the whole point.

Jesus clearly defined His attitude toward serving each other by His example of foot washing. "Now that I, your Lord and Teacher, have washed your feet, you also should wash one another's feet. I have set you an example that you should do as I have done for you" (John 13:14-15).

Foot washing was an activity for servants. It was messy (and I would imagine not a little unpleasant, considering there was nothing like body wash and extra strength deodorant back then). Jesus had no business washing people's feet. Why would He do that when He could perform miracles?

It's clear that Jesus wanted to set an example for us. Servanthood is not always easy or enjoyable. It isn't always convenient; sometimes it's downright messy. But God encourages us all to have a servant's heart.

Prayer for Today

Dear God, give me a heart to give pleasure and relaxation to my mate without expecting anything in return.

Project Reports

"Let me tell you about the spa day we had at our house while the kids were at school. A professional masseuse (someone we know, so it wasn't weird) came over to our house, brought her massage table, chocolate-covered strawberries, sparkling apple cider, calming music, and robes for us to wear. She gave both of us a nice long massage while the other relaxed and rested. It was soooo relaxing, and I would highly recommend it."
—Kelli

Your Plan for the Project *(copy your plan on the Project Planner at the back of this book)*

Results *(mate's reaction, my reaction)*

Project 9

It's All About Her
Love, Love, Love

"You may choose your words like a connoisseur,
And polish it up with art,
But the word that sways, and stirs, and stays,
Is the word that comes from the heart."

—ELLA WHEELER WILCOX

Your Project

Simple. Men, write down 12 things you love about your wife. (I said simple, not easy.) Pray for her right now, thanking God for her qualities. Also leave a note where she'll find it (even a sticky note on the grocery list), one that speaks about her qualities.

Some of the things your wife may appreciate hearing:

- I love you because you're always thinking about how to support me.

- I love you because you're kind to everyone you meet.

- I love you because you know my faults and love me anyway.

- I love you because you don't mind giving me my guy time every once in a while.

- I love you because you treat me with respect in front of the kids.

- I love you because you make me laugh.
- I love you because you challenge me to be my best in every area.

Now it's your turn:

1.

2.

3.

4.

5.

6.

7.

8.

9.

10.

11.

12.

Purpose of the Project

Encouragement

As a wife, I need to hear regularly why my husband loves me. As a husband, you're the only one who can give that gift to your wife. Be the encouragement she needs you to be today.

We have such power when it comes to encouraging those God has put in our path.

God has put an important person in my life, one I'll graciously say "tests" me frequently. No judgment here; I'm sure the feeling is mutual much of the time. I don't have a choice whether to be around her, so I decided it was time to take a little direct action and perform an experiment. (I'll do anything that's emotionally healthy and pleasing to God, as long as I can dress it up as a party game or fun activity.)

In the spirit of trying something fun, I deliberately said five encouraging things a day for seven days to this person. Whether I felt like it or not. Whether I thought she deserved it or not.

Sometimes it's a real stretch—"Wow, I really like that font at the bottom of your email signature"—but I'm forcing myself, nonetheless.

This is not a "fake it till you make it" proposition. I'm not trying to be disingenuous with my compliments and praise. The problem is not so much with this person, but with a pattern in my own thinking. I've realized that as soon as she walks through the door, my brain immediately jumps to the place where I catalog all the irritating and annoying things she does.

The more I encourage my friend, the easier it becomes. Not only am I becoming more conscious about all of the good qualities she has, I can see her making an effort in our relationship as well.

Sometimes I'm loath to give out encouragement, but I need to let the realization take root that:

> "Everyone who has ever done a kind deed for us, or spoken one word of encouragement to us, has entered into the make-up of our character and of our thoughts, as well as our success."
>
> —George Matthew Adams

1. *People are dying for encouragement.* Proverbs 12:25 says, "Anxiety weighs down the heart, but a kind word cheers it up." We have the power to help heal people with our words. We have no right to be stingy with our praise when there is a world in need of encouragement.

2. *Encouraging others heals us.* While I know the effects on my

friend are adding up, I'm the one who benefits from giving encouragement. It's exhausting to be irritated by a person, everyday. But when we train our minds to seek out the good, and then express it, we don't heal just the people around us; we also receive healing. We can be restored and relieved from our previous repetitive and damaging thoughts. Thomas Jefferson said, "You are not what you think you are. You are what you think." Help someone today by encouraging them and, trust me, the benefits will be yours.

Prayer for Today

Dear God, make me a blessing to my spouse in my actions *and* my words.

Getting Creative

- If this is an especially challenging time in your marriage, it may be hard to come up with reasons why you love someone. Now may be the time to ask God to bring to mind the reasons you fell in love in the first place. Write them down as you remember.

- Get your wife to see this list any way that you want. It can be as simple as reading it aloud to her tonight, sending her an email of this list, or placing the book (open to this chapter) somewhere she'll find it.

Project Reports

"This was a really good project for us as it led us into a much bigger conversation—one that we never would have had without *Happy Habits for Every Couple*. We discussed why we love each other and gave what I consider fairly standard responses for a married couple in our stage of life. But then we went even deeper—about how even through the ups and downs of life, there isn't anyone else we'd want to share it with. We reaffirmed our absolute love for each other, talked about the day-to-day things that detract from us showing the depth of our love to each other, and talked about ways to show more consistently how much we truly do love each other. Lastly, we agreed we're still happy that we chose each other when we got married six years ago!"—Kristin

Your Plan for the Project *(copy your plan on the Project Planner at the back of this book)*

Results *(mate's reaction, my reaction)*

Project 10

Bella Notte
Have a Treat by Candlelight

"After a good dinner, one can forgive
anybody, even one's own relatives."
OSCAR WILDE

Your Project

Eat together by candlelight.

Purpose of the Project

It was one of those movies that I didn't mind watching with my kids. (The fact that it never had a purple dinosaur helped greatly.) *Lady and the Tramp*, originally released by Disney in 1955, was Disney at its best. Great songs ("He's a Tramp"), great villains (those nasty Siamese cats, Si and Am), and a great plot (star-crossed lovers, each from different sides of the tracks). What's not to love?

Of course, everyone remembers the scene when Tramp takes Lady on their first date, and they hit the Italian cafe. There's music (the romantic "Bella Notte," sung by Tony), there's candlelight, and there's a big plate of spaghetti. While the "spaghetti kiss" is oh-so-cute, the part that really gets me is when Tramp, seeing there's only one meatball left, uses his snout to nudge it toward Lady for her to enjoy.

Now that's my kind of man.

Making Candlelight Moments Happen

This is one of those projects my husband and I had a hard time getting around to. We knew it was important to schedule it since it was one of those "important but not urgent" items on our long list of things-to-do.

When it was time to actually do the project, our conversation went something like this:

"Where are the candles?"

"Do you know where the lighter is?"

"Don't we have a box of matches with the camping stuff?"

"Oh, never mind."

And then, one Saturday, the romance was forced upon us. We woke up very late that morning. Roger had a board meeting at church, which he slept through. (Who schedules a board meeting at six o'clock on a Saturday morning? It's enough to make a man switch denominations.) It turns out that not only had his alarm clock lost power, the whole neighborhood was without even a flicker of a coffeepot.

> We need to unplug—literally and figuratively—every once in a while to keep the romance alive.

At first, it was kind of fun. We slept late and made alternate plans for the day. My 16-year-old Kimberly remarked, "Wow, it feels just like a pioneer family." (I didn't want to ruin the mood by pointing out that the average pioneer family didn't have indoor plumbing or cell phones.)

So, after some discussion of the day's new plans, we drove through the local Starbucks for breakfast (that is what Laura Ingalls would have done, right?) and spent the day running errands.

We got back home at 6:00 p.m., and still no flicker from even one DVR.

Roger and I looked at each other wondering what to do next. It was pretty pathetic. We had no clue what to do without the aid of laptops, big screen TVs, and microwave ovens. We had become *that* couple.

So, we had no choice but to get creative. If necessity is the mother of invention, then desperation is the father of creativity. We dug through our camping equipment and found the lanterns among the gear from our annual "Vacation—Unplugged." We pulled out the grill and cooked sausages and potatoes, lit a fire in the outdoor pit, and talked for about four hours.

As much as we like to eat outdoors, four hours is a little long to be gazing into each other's eyes. The truth is, nobody whooped louder than I did when the electric company repaired the cable so the lights (and computers and TVs) flittered back to life.

It was a good reminder that we need to unplug—literally and figuratively—every once in a while to keep the romance alive.

Prayer for Today

God, help me to pull back from my routine to focus on what is important—You and my partner—for a few moments every day.

Getting Creative

- My husband and I enjoy a different version of dining-by-candlelight—tapas by tiki torches. We love to eat outside by the outdoor fireplace; sometimes we just light a few tiki torches for ambience.

- Another way to create the atmosphere you're looking for: use twinkle lights, found at any good hardware store. Whether you string them in the trees, over your back patio, or in the bushes, turning them on at night delivers "romance" for less than 20 bucks. (A quick caveat here: If your twinkle lights are red and green and have been up since December 5, they're not a mood enhancer. It's possible they just might provoke a different kind of feeling as your spouse asks you, once again, to *puleeze* take down the Christmas lights.)

Project Reports

"This was a nice treat for us, not so much because of the food, but because it got us out of our normal evening routine—dinner with the kids, baths, etc.—and forced us to spend some 'sweet' time together. It was a nice way to be cute and cuddly without having to do anything major!"—Kristina

"We were on vacation, so I packed two small candles and some matches in my suitcase so that we could have our candlelight night together. I think that my wife was more excited that I planned ahead than about the romance!"—Rod

Your Plan for the Project *(copy your plan on the Project Planner at the back of this book)*

Results *(mate's reaction, my reaction)*

Project 11

It's All About Him
R-E-S-P-E-C-T—What It Means to Him

*"Only those who respect the personality of
others can be of real use to them."*
ALBERT SCHWEITZER

Your Project

Ladies, it's your turn. Write down the reasons you respect
your husband or are proud of him, and then make sure he
sees the list.

Just a few examples of some things you could write:

- I respect you because I feel protected by you.
- I am proud of how you handle yourself in life.
- I'm proud of you because you take care of our family by working hard.
- I respect you because of the ways you're growing more Christ-like every day.
- I respect you because you take care of yourself physically.
- I'm proud of you because you're a great dad.
- I respect you because you respect me in the way that you speak to me.

Now it's time to come up with your own:

1.

2.

3.

4.

5.

6.

7.

8.

9.

10.

11.

12.

Purpose of the Project

There are times I don't want to be nice to my husband. We had a fight. He said things. I said things. I know what buttons to push and when to push them.

I don't always mean to pick a fight, but sometimes the pressure is so great, it feels like I have to relieve it one way or another. Sadly, it's usually the people I love the most who end up in the midst of my explosion.

It's not about respecting your husband only if you feel like it. It's about acting respectfully around your husband, even when you don't feel like it or think he deserves it.

My actions toward others reflect the level of respect I have for Christ. It's because I am loved by God that I need to be respectful to everyone—even when I don't feel like it.

In *The Politically Incorrect Wife*, authors Nancy Cobb and Connie

Grigsby talk about the importance of having respect for your husband, no matter the circumstance:

> Survey after survey tells us that a woman's greatest desire in marriage is to feel loved by her husband, while a man's number one desire is to be respected by his wife. Respect must be one of the more difficult traits for wives to exhibit. Both Peter and Paul mention it: "And the wife must see to it that she respects her husband" (Ephesians 5:33 NASB).
>
> A wife's respect is shown by highly regarding her husband. Often women withhold respect from their husband, feeling that their husbands don't deserve it. "When he starts doing such and so," many women say, "then I'll give him my respect."
>
> When a woman does this, what she is doing is rewriting the Bible. Notice that it doesn't say, "Wives, see to it that you respect your husbands if they deserve it." It says, "Wives respect your husbands." It is a directive. Wives must choose whether they will respect their husbands. Do you respect your husband conditionally? Do you manipulate him to do certain things before you will give him your respect? Are you still waiting for him to change, thinking that then you will respect him? Remember, respect is not something your husband must earn from you. It is something you must give him because of the role God gave him.

> As a husband's love must be unconditional, so must a wife's respect be unconditional.

As a husband's love must be unconditional, so must a wife's respect be unconditional. I thank God that my husband's love for me does not depend on how he feels about my actions and behavior that day. If that were the case, there would be a couple of days every month, like clockwork, where I would not be "feelin' the love."

Some Ways to Show Respect

One of the pieces of instruction that writers are told over and over is "Show, don't tell." Simply, that means when you're writing about a man eating a hamburger, don't write, "The man liked hamburgers." Instead, write, "Joe couldn't help but pant just a little as the burger came off the grill. He placed it carefully inside the bun, and then added his delicate balance of spicy mustard and ketchup, his grilled (never raw) purple onions, and exactly three slices of dill pickle. Watching Joe prepare his hamburger is like watching a master artisan at work."

Now, which of those two descriptions makes you want a burger tonight?

It's the same with respect. It's great to tell your husband how much you respect him (in fact, it is imperative), but it's just as important to *show* him how much you respect him.

Here are some ways to show respect:

- When you disagree with a decision or an opinion of his, discuss it in private (and definitely not in front of his friends, family, or kids).

- Keep from arguing with him or tossing out not-so-subtle digs in front of others.

- Brag on him in front of people that he cares about.

- Defer to him on decisions that are important to him but not as important to you.

Prayer for Today

Dear God, thank You for my husband. Help me to respect him in all that I say and do.

Getting Creative

- Put the list somewhere that he will find it in private—his nightstand, his briefcase, in the bathroom.

- Write it on a separate piece of paper and put it up on the bathroom mirror.

- Put those reasons on separate sticky notes and leave them places he will find them throughout the day (his lunch sack, his car, his gym bag).

Project Reports

"At the beginning I read through all the daily projects and thought to myself, *No way. How can I find twelve things I respect about him after the betrayal?* Well, I prayed God would reveal attributes I respected and liked about my husband, and I was truly surprised to come up with eight. I'm hoping you get the picture. If we're willing to allow God into our hearts and use us as His vessels, He can turn brokenness into something beautiful. I'm not here to tell you that we're at the point we'd like to be—but we're in a much better place than we were when we began *Happy Habits*."—Barb

"I really enjoyed taking the time to write things down. Whether it was a sweet note or a list of things we love/ respect, I like having to think enough to put things into written words. We don't often do that anymore, and I enjoyed doing it a lot."—Christina

Your Plan for the Project *(copy your plan on the Project Planner at the back of this book)*

Results *(mate's reaction, my reaction)*

Project 12

Lingerie

"If love is blind, why is lingerie so popular?"
Source Unknown

Your Project

Ladies, your job is to either dig out or shop for a piece of lingerie and then wear it to bed. Guys, don't think you're getting off without an assignment today. It's your job to make sure your wife knows throughout the day that you're looking forward to your time together, as well as making her feel as cherished as possible.

Purpose of the Project

Girls, let's start with you.

I want you to kick it up just a notch. If you haven't worn lingerie in a while (or ever), I'm not asking you to go look for a bustier and thigh-high fishnet stockings with a garter belt. But if you run around in a holey "Frankie Says Relax!" T-shirt circa 1984, it's time to let your husband see you in something that's designed to be peek-a-boo (instead of having become that way from old age).

Talk with your husband about what he would like, and then compromise between that and what you feel comfortable in. I want you to feel beautiful, not worried about a thong that's getting caught in places fabric was never intended to be.

Guys—now it's your turn.

It's hard for us girls to feel sexy when we're distracted by everything else in life. The dishes need to be done, the kids are awake, and oh, by the way, I feel fat today. So your job is to do something today to help us transition from mommy/employee to your lingerie-clad roommate.

So guys, start the morning by telling us how much you're looking forward to our time together. When you get home, pitch in with the kids and flirt a little bit over dinner. Your wife needs to understand that you care about what she cares about, that you want to make this a time of connection and intimacy (with a lot of fun and flirting, as well).

> Your husband is designed by God to enjoy seeing you scantily clad, and you're the only one who can allow him to enjoy this very special, fun, and flirty experience.

As I mentioned before, part of our church's experience with *Happy Habits* included a celebration of what God had done in the lives and marriages of the people of our church. It was a Sunday evening, and everyone was posting slips of paper on the walls telling about the miracles God had performed during the project. As I read over the praises, I couldn't hold back the tears of gratitude over what God had done.

And then I got to my favorite praise of all. On this purple piece of paper, a man had simply written, "God, thank You for lingerie. For the first time in our marriage, my wife wore lingerie. AWESOME."

Now that was a David-style cry-out-to-God kind of praise.

In a great healthy marriage, lingerie is something that a husband can enjoy only on his wife. No ogling Victoria's Secret catalogs. So wives, you cannot hold out on your man.

Imagine, ladies, if you will, that in some strange set of circumstances your husband gained control over the world's supply of chocolate. Godiva, Hershey's, and Ghirardelli were all under your man's control. Imagine if you were around it every day—smelling it, seeing it—and he never let you have any.

That is how it is with your husband and lingerie. He is designed by God to enjoy seeing you scantily clad, and you're the only one who can allow your husband to enjoy this very special, fun, and flirty experience. Husbands, you're the only one who can let us know that you love the effort we're putting into this.

Whenever I speak at conferences about the importance of wearing the good stuff for your man, invariably some size four will come up to me afterward and say something along the lines of, "I used to wear lingerie, but since I had kids, I just don't feel comfortable with my body anymore." I look at the Mary-Kate and Ashley clone standing in front of me and think, *Yeah, I am not real comfortable with your body right now either. Perhaps you should take a step back.*

I know, I know—jealous much?

But if my size-four friend feels uncomfortable in lingerie, what chance do the rest of us have?

> Sometimes I just need to "shut up and suit up." He is worth it.

I found out after talking to dozens of men that most guys are not looking for perfection—they're looking for effort. They want to know that they are worth the effort we make to shave our legs and put on something frilly and potentially uncomfortable.

I have also heard (and used) all the excuses for why women don't want to wear lingerie:

- "It makes me feel sleazy." *That is listening to the world's view of your sexual relationship, not how God created you to enjoy each other. Again, we are not talking fishnet stockings and a black peek-a-boo merry widow. Find something pretty that makes you feel fabulous. And if you are still embarrassed, take a bold friend along on your shopping trip who can be brave enough to talk you into something gorgeous.*

- "It costs too much."—*Honey, if you can buy it at Target, it doesn't cost too much.*

- "I'm pregnant."—*Most maternity stores carry lingerie. So unless you are in your third trimester and about to give birth, there is no excuse.*

- "I'm too fat."—*Lingerie comes in all sizes. Don't wait (or make your husband wait) until you get down to the perfect weight. Take care of your body and let your husband enjoy it at the same time.*

- "It's such a waste—it only stays on for five minutes."—*Um, that's how you know it's working. Besides, as our friend Steve says, "Yes, it may stay on for only five minutes, but the memories last a lifetime."*

I know all the excuses. I have used all the excuses. But knowing how important this is to my husband, sometimes I just need to "shut up and suit up." He is worth it.

Getting Creative

- Guys, whatever your wife is wearing, make sure she knows that you appreciate the effort and that you adore how beautiful she looks.

- Girls, you may want to get fitted for something special. Most shops have someone on staff to discreetly measure you and suggest which items would look best on you. If that's too far outside your comfort zone, how about taking along a trusted friend (the kind you would trust with the PIN to your debit card)?

- If finances allow, buy a couple of items to start (or add to) your lingerie wardrobe.

- Stash your purchase in the master bath and surprise your guy by coming out fully—that is, partially—dressed. Double-check the lock on the bedroom door to make sure it's secure. You want your husband to be the only one surprised.

- Oh, and if you don't have a lock on the bedroom door—are you kidding me? Get one installed immediately.

Prayer for Today

God, thanks for making so many ways for me to enjoy my spouse.

Project Reports

"I was out of town on this project day, but I still wanted the checkmark, so I went shopping for something pretty that I could wear later in the week. That morning I called my husband to let him know we could check off that day's project. He called me back a couple of hours later to say that he hadn't been able to concentrate at work all day since he knew I had been shopping that morning. I would call that a completely successful project."—Marie

Your Plan for the Project *(copy your plan on the Project Planner at the back of this book)*

Results *(mate's reaction, your reaction)*

Project 13

Check Mates and Check Marks
Getting the Job Done

"He gives strength to the weary
and increases the power of the weak."
ISAIAH 40:29

Your Project

Discuss and decide on a home project to complete and erase
off both of your to-do lists.

Purpose of the Project

While some couples bond over long romantic walks along the
beach and candlelit dinners, I lean toward the romance method
employed by my friends Judy and David.

I was fortunate enough to stay at Judy and David's home during
a round of speaking I was doing in Oregon. When they moved from
the Bay Area of Northern California to Grants Pass, Oregon, they
bought a home to provide a retreat for people in ministry to refresh
and relax. They call their home "Sheep's Rest."

What makes this couple even more amazing (besides their gorgeous home and generosity) is that Judy performs all these acts of
hospitality without legs. Judy is a double amputee who writes and
speaks around the world about the restoration God has performed
through many miracles in her life. There's very little in life that Judy
doesn't do: she's an avid swimmer, makes some mean Mexican food,
travels the world delivering and repairing wheelchairs, and has given
birth to and raised three beautiful daughters.

While all that is incredible enough, the thing that really blew my mind is how she kept her house so clean. (Yes, I am so very easily impressed.)

I could not believe all that Judy was able to do during my stay. When I arrived the floors were freshly shined and the pillows fluffed. Despite having two adorable dachshunds, there was nary a dog hair to be found. I know that managing a much smaller house takes all the time and energy I can muster (and still I never seem to get everything off the kitchen floor). I was amazed at how Judy was able to manage it all. I simply had to know.

"Judy, I have a much smaller house, not to mention two legs." (Judy is the kind of friend you can say such things to.) "How do you take care of this huge house?"

"I manage pretty well—after all, it's just David and me and the two dogs. But yesterday morning at breakfast David said, 'Judy, I know that Kathi is coming today, and there are things you want to get done. So today, my day is your day. Let me know what you want to get done, and I'll do it.'"

I just sat and stared for a minute. Finally, I found the words to express what I was feeling, "That is the most romantic thing I have ever heard in my life."

Why do I find a sparkling kitchen floor so hot? Some of us are just wired that way.

Yep, you can bring me flowers, you can sing me love songs, but if you really want to declare your undying love for me, wipe down the shelves in the fridge.

Our differing styles of "fun" is why one of the most romantic things that Roger can do for me is to work with me on cleaning the garage, cooking meals for a month in advance, or scrubbing down every inch of the bathroom with Clorox.

> If you really want to declare your undying love for me, wipe down the shelves in the fridge.

I really do believe this is how many people are wired. We experience a great sense of accomplishment by checking things off a list. Sure, a weekend at a resort would be great, but two dozen meals prepared and labeled in the freezer? Priceless.

I love the feeling of accomplishment I get when Roger and I work on a project together. We combine his outside-the-box thinking with my "Yes, but we have to be able to live with it" thinking in order to get the best results for the project.

If your partner is not a project kind of person, avoid overwhelming him or her with a huge undertaking. Keep the project for this day manageable so everyone enjoys that feeling of accomplishment without being weighed down.

If your partner *is* the project kind of person, realize that the way to his heart may not be through his stomach—it may be by vacuuming out his car.

Finding the Energy to Get it All Done

Research subjects at the University of Virginia were making mountains out of molehills.

In an experiment researchers had students stand at the bottom of various hills and estimate the angle of the slope. The students consistently overestimated the difficulty of the hill. For example, state law in Virginia prohibits any roads with a grade greater than 9 degrees, and yet the students estimated steep roads to be 25 degrees or more. The overestimations increased dramatically when the students were carrying something heavy.

When we're burdened, it's easy to become overwhelmed merely by anticipating the effort we'll need to expend, whether it's loving our spouse, committing to a quiet time, or engaging in something like *Happy Habits for Every Couple.*

But God is faithful to give us the strength to complete those things that honor Him.

Prayer for Today

Dear God, please don't let me rely on my own strength but to always rely on You.

Getting Creative

Can't think of anything to check off your list? Here are a couple of ideas to get you started:

- Clean out both of your cars. Detail with the Shop-Vac.
- Plant a Salsa Garden. All you need are a few tomato plants, some chilies, cilantro, basil, oregano, and green onions.
- Match all the stray socks in the house.
- Cook ahead for a week and put some frozen meals in the freezer.
- Clean out a section of the garage.

Project Reports

"We did things a little differently and swapped off things that we could do for the other person, but did them in the same room. He set up and networked my computer, and I ironed a bunch of his shirts. It was nice to be in the same room and chatting with each other, knowing we were both helping each other out."—Tom and Karie

"I had been dreading cleaning out the garage because I never know what I can throw out and what I can't. It was great to work together and make decisions together. I finally was able to get rid of the golf clubs that had been sitting in the garage, untouched, since before we were married (12 years ago!). I feel lighter!"—Sue

Your Plan for the Project *(copy your plan on the Project Planner at the back of this book)*

Results *(mate's reaction, my reaction)*

Project 14

Candlelight Weather Report
Carve Out Some Time
to Just Sit and Talk Over Your Day

Piglet sidled up to Pooh from behind. "Pooh!" he whispered.
"Yes, Piglet?"
"Nothing," said Piglet, taking Pooh's paw.
"I just wanted to be sure of you."

A.A. MILNE

Your Project

Take some time to just sit and be. Light a candle, sit down
together, and give your spouse an "emotional weather report."
Reciprocate by asking what was the best thing that happened
during his or her day. What was the worst thing? Then ask
your spouse for any prayer requests.

Purpose of the Project

"I feel like we've known each other forever..."

If you've been dating for three weeks and make the statement
above, don't be surprised if the people sitting with you, who have
been married since you were watching *The Brady Bunch* in your footie
pajamas, have a hard time controlling their gag reflex.

While Roger and I have known each other as friends and ministry
partners for over 20 years, we have been married for only 10. And
while we know each other better than we know anyone else on the
planet, we still have a lot to learn.

161

Yes, I know Roger's hopes and dreams for his career, our family, and his relationship with God. Yes, he knows my addiction to shoes, bags, and books, and usually finds that addiction, if not adorable, downright tolerable.

But there are ways of knowing a person that come only from time and experience.

Some of the experiences that Roger and I have been through together that have helped us "know and be known":

- Planning a wedding
- Picking out paint colors
- Raising teenagers
- Going through a major financial crisis
- Traveling
- Reading a map while traveling
- Refinancing our home

Some adventures that we have yet to enjoy as a married couple that would undoubtedly give us new insights into each other:

- Buying a car
- Buying a house
- Going through a major illness
- Painting a room together
- Losing a job

It is only by going through life together, praying for each other, supporting one another when it's not fun or convenient, that we can forge the relationship that will take us through the "till death do us part" part of marriage.

Senior Moment Accompanied by Googly Eyes

Is there anything better in the world than seeing a couple qualified to be card-carrying members of the AARP making googly eyes at each other? That couple represents a lot of life lived, a lot of grace given, and a lot of putting the needs of their spouse before their own. They have more than earned the right to embarrass their children (and grandchildren) with public displays of affection.

My friend Cathy has been married to her husband, Ed, for 40 years. Whenever she's asked at a bridal shower what her marital advice is, she has the same words of wisdom, "Never stop being kind to each other." Cathy and Ed still meet each other for lunch, surprise each other with weekend trips, and regularly make time for each other. It sounds simple and trite, but Ed and Cathy take time to be kind to each other.

In looking around at the marriages we come in contact with everyday, it seems that some simple and trite might be in order.

> While we know each other better than we know anyone else on the planet, we still have a lot to learn.

If your lives are running in completely different directions, it's time to carve out some couple time. Check in with each other. Find out how that bonehead at your wife's work is behaving himself. Ask your husband about the project that's kept him up late at night. If you have kids, keep it a "kid-talk-free zone," even if just for a few minutes.

Prayer for Today

God, I want to know and be known by my spouse.

Getting Creative

- Ask your spouse what kind of day she had.
- What was the best thing that happened to him yesterday?
- What was the worst thing that happened to her yesterday?
- Is there something specific you can pray for?

- Also, think of ways to help relieve some of his stress or make him laugh.

Your Plan for the Project *(copy your plan on the Project Planner at the back of this book)*

Results *(mate's reaction, my reaction)*

Date Your Mate

Do Something You Enjoyed Before You Got Married

"Love is a friendship set to music."
E. Joseph Cossman

Your Project

Do some activity that you enjoyed when you had all the time in the world for each other. Walk on the beach, have a movie marathon, or see how many of the 31 flavors you can mix into one bowl.

Purpose of the Project

Roger and I had known each other for years before we got married. In fact, when I was in college, I earned money for a missions trip by doing childcare at his church (he loves to tell people that he married the babysitter).

But it wasn't until we started dating that we really got to know each other—finding out what kind of movies I liked, how spicy he liked his Thai food (very), and all the things each of us liked to do for hobbies.

Eventually, the questioning got around to one of Roger's favorite activities—camping and all its variations (hiking, cooking over an open fire, and so on).

I've never been much of an "outdoors kind of girl." I worked long hard hours at my job in order to ensure that I got to sleep indoors. I'm not really fond of food with dirt in it. The appeal of camping was lost on me.

But I was in the midst of a dilemma. While I was not one for camping, I was falling in love with this guy. If Roger wanted to go on a hike, I knew I would love just being with him.

> While we're dating, we try hard to be the dream companion for our future mate. And then we get married.

So when Roger asked if I liked camping, I may have exaggerated...just a bit.

"Camping? I *love* camping! My friends call me Camping Kathi. They call it the great outdoors for a reason!"

So sue me. I was falling in love.

Plus, don't tell me that some of you guys didn't profess to enjoy shopping for shoes with your girl before you got hitched. You carried her purse while she tried on clothes, and there was never the mention of the word *budget* when you were wooing her.

My friend Sara was dating Tom, who eventually became her husband. When they were in the early stages of falling in love, Sara was concerned about how she was going to keep up with Tom's love of all things 49ers. At the time, Steve Young was the team's quarterback, and Tom had season tickets. He ate, slept, and breathed everything Niners. So Sara became a die-hard fan. Before attending a game (or even watching one on Steve's 543-inch Jumbotron), she studied the players' names and bought a team jersey to wear to the first game. The day before the big game, however, Sara admitted to me that she was nervous.

"I just don't want to make a fool of myself in front of him. I just don't know that much about baseball."

We all do it.

While we're dating, we try hard to be the dream companion for our future mate. If he loves *Star Wars* movies (all six of them) we love

Star Wars movies (all...gulp...six of them). If she wants to watch movies where Jennifer Aniston gets her man, he's in the seat next to her, holding the popcorn.

And then we get married.

Suddenly, all the romance that was so abundant while we were dating is pushed aside to deal with kids and home repairs, jobs and paying bills. (Funny, Visa doesn't care how much we're in love. They want their money, and now.)

So when Roger asked me to join him to watch boy movies, there were always dishes needing to be washed or emails waiting to be answered. I didn't need to see John McClane save another thing from blowing up during another *Die Hard* movie. I needed to figure out what we were having for dinner tomorrow.

But part of the reason we got married is so we would have someone to do all those things we love with. I'm glad I don't have to wait by the phone to see if that cute guy from the bookstore is going to call for a Friday night date. I have a permanent Friday night date.

And while I may have the guy, if we don't work hard at it, we won't have the date. It's worth hiring the babysitter. It's worth going to a movie that isn't your favorite. It's worth it to remember what you liked to do before dating and how far you have come.

Why It's Important to Remember Where We Have Been

After just a few months of marriage, I felt as though my husband and I were losing some of the connectedness. We were stressed about kids, stressed about money, and stressed about life in general. There were even a few times I wondered if getting married had been the right decision.

As I was relating this to a friend, she gently reminded me of all the ways God had confirmed that Roger and I were supposed to be together. She explained how important it is to have reminders in our life about how far God has brought us—just as Samuel set up a reminder for the people of Israel when God rescued them from their Philistine oppressors: "Then Samuel took a stone and set it up between

Mizpah and Shen. He named it Ebenezer, saying, 'Thus far the LORD has helped us'" (1 Samuel 7:12).

Physical reminders of God's love and provision are important in our lives. Whether it's rocks in our garden, diaries filled with a record of God's miracles in our lives, or photo albums containing reminders of His blessings, it's important to make sure we keep track of God's blessings in our lives. That way, when He feels distant, we have reminders that God is concerned for our every thought and need.

Prayer for Today

Dear God, please don't let us forget that You are writing our romance, every day. Remind us of Your great plans for our marriage.

Getting Creative

- Incorporate...
  - Songs that were popular while you were dating
  - Food you enjoyed before you both watched each other's waistlines grow
  - Movies you watched while you were dating
- Create your own playlist—the songs you both love that tell the story of your relationship. Burn a CD or make it an iPod list.
- If you're a parent of young children, babysitting is required.
- Your activity doesn't have to be exotic or expensive. It might even be something as simple as hanging out in a bookstore, which my husband and I both love doing. Maybe you, too, would enjoy hitting Barnes & Noble without tripping over toddlers in the children's section.
- The longer we are married, the shorter our dates become. Make sure you don't have work planned for when you get home. Take a little time to linger over each other.

Your Plan for the Project *(copy your plan on the Project Planner at the back of this book)*

Results *(your mate's reaction, your reaction)*

Sex

Having "The Talk"

*"Don't have sex, man. It leads to kissing and pretty
soon you have to start talking to them."*
STEVE MARTIN

Your Bonus Project

This week I want you to kick it up a notch. Throughout the
week, I want you to have some conversations about sex. And
no, not while you are under the covers.

Is there a time that you can talk about sex
when there isn't the pressure to perform? I want
you to be able to at least broach the subject of
what is working in this area of your relationship (and offering generous amounts of praise
for that) as well as other areas where maybe you
would like to explore a little.

Some areas that can be up for discussion:

- Massage
- Lingerie
- Foreplay
- Romance
- Frequency
- Variety

Ask your
partner what
he or she wants
to see out
of your sex life.
Make it fun,
supportive,
and flirty.

This is an excellent time to figure out what is working for you as a couple and where you would like to try something new.

Make sure that you go into this conversation, not with your own agenda, but asking your partner what he or she wants to see out of your sex life. Make it fun, supportive, and flirty.

Whenever Roger and I have a tough area in our marriage to discuss, we usually head over to our local bookstore or hop onto Amazon to find a book on the subject. If your sexual relationship is a difficult area in your marriage, may I suggest *Red-Hot Monogamy* by Bill and Pam Farrel? This is a fun and nonthreatening book that will give you a way to discuss this sensitive area with a lot of love and support.

Prayer for Today

Dear God, help us to be open, honest, and kind as we talk about this important area of our relationship.

Your Plan for the Project *(copy your plan on the Project Planner at the back of this book)*

Results *(mate's reaction, my reaction)*

Week Three Projects

Project 15

Look to the Example of Others
Who Do You Admire? And Why?

*"I have always been an admirer. I regard the gift of
admiration as indispensable if one is to amount to
something; I don't know where I would be without it."*
Thomas Mann

Your Project

Today, as a couple, think about some of the other couples
you know. Write down some things you admire about them
and why. Pray for them right now. Also, take a moment to
email, call, or write a note telling them what you admire
about their marriage.

If you want to become a better golfer, your best plan is to hang
out with people who know more than you do about the game. If you
want to learn Japanese, you better find yourself some native speakers.
And if you want to have a great marriage, you need to learn from
those around you who have been at it a while—and still love each
other well.

Purpose of the Project

You might have had parents who did the whole wedding vow thing
right. They loved, they honored, and they cherished each other. Dad
showered love and affection on Mom, and Mom always spoke highly

of Dad. They stayed together and loved each other "until death do us part."

Congratulations—you're one of the lucky ones.

Most couples don't have the benefit of two sets of parents who modeled godly love in their marriage. That's why it's so critical to have other role models in your life—couples whose marriages you can draw from. So I encourage you to look around for people in your life who are doing it right, and model yourself after them.

> Look around for people in your life who are doing it right, and model yourself after them.

This is not unlike any other skill you attempt to learn. You look to people with a good technique—a successful approach—and model yourself after them. Because I'm always working to improve as a writer, I hang out with other writers who are better than I am and have been doing it longer. These are women with multiple books under their belts who know the triumphs and trials of getting words on paper. It doesn't matter that they write in a style different from mine, or that they've been writing for so much longer than I have. It's great having women in my life who have simultaneously faced teenage drivers and writer's block and have lived to tell the tale—and can encourage me to do the same.

When I hang out with women who are good at the whole marriage thing (and who not only have survived but actually enjoy their marriage), it makes me see the power I have to make changes in my own relationship.

Recently, Roger and I went out to dinner with a couple that has been married for over 25 years. Since we've known Jim and Sue for over 15 of those years, it's been amazing to see that, while they have changed and grown over the years, their intentional dedication to each other has remained strong. It was a good reminder of our need as a couple to stay focused on putting our relationship before our personal desires.

Here are some of the couples that Roger and I look to as examples for our own marriage:

Jim and Kim

Jim was a pastor to both Roger and me before we were married. What we loved about Jim and Kim's marriage was the show of support they offered each other. Kim encouraged Jim as he went to school while he was the senior pastor of a church, and Jim was there for Kim as she led the outreach ministry of their growing congregation. It's not easy being a pastor—or a pastor's wife—so Jim and Kim had to be fervent and intentional about encouraging each other. They're definitely an example Roger and I want to follow as we both pursue our own passions.

Sherry and Terrin

On Saturday mornings you can often find Terrin, Sherry, and their three kids (and some of their assorted friends) building lighting walls or swinging from our church's baptismal, draping fabric. No, they're not setting up an elaborate practical joke for the Sunday service. Sherry is in charge of set design at our church, and when one of the family members is involved in something, all the members get roped into service. And the amazing thing is, they actually enjoy it. What we love about this couple is their complete and utter dedication to leading and loving their family. Their kids have a heart for service because their parents do. Terrin and Sherry have a close relationship with their three teenagers because they work at it—every day.

Pam and John

What is so lovely about this couple is that after years of marriage (they are grandparents multiple times now) they still have an unfailing love for each other. They know each other's "challenges" (in a less healthy marriage, we would call them faults) and have a great sense of humor about them. Not only do they speak well of each other in public, they get downright googly-eyed about the other. Their pride for each other is clear.

Even if you had great parents as examples of a solid and healthy marriage, it's a good idea to look at some of the other couples you know and draw on the best from each of them. It's up to each of us to cobble together our own mosaics, examples of what God wants from our marriage.

Leaving an Everyday Legacy

Are you one of those couples who has it going on? You demonstrate love to each other regularly, you speak respectfully about each other (whether your partner is standing next to you or not), and you cheer each other on and are invested in each other.

If you're one of those couples, let me encourage you. Your legacy means more than you will ever know while you're here on earth. Not only will your family be blessed for generations to come, but also the other couples that you interact with—at church, at work, in your neighborhood—are witnessing living proof that there's a different way to live. You're demonstrating that wives don't need to be caustic or biting in order to get their points across. You're demonstrating that real men love their wives and reciprocate respect and love to them without losing themselves.

Prayer for Today

Dear God, thank You for bringing _____ (other couple) into our lives. Thank You for the example they have been before us, and help us to be a godly example before others.

Getting Creative

- Think about your and your spouse's parents. What qualities did you admire in their marriage? What are some of the things you'd like to mirror in your own marriage?

- Think about some of the other couples you know. What are some of the qualities they have that you would like to see in your own marriage? Perhaps...

  — They speak well of each other, building each other up.

  — They laugh together easily, but never at each other.

  — They are always looking to the needs of their partner first.

  — They flirt with each other.

Project Reports

"It was nice to have that discussion and to try to emulate those things in our own day-to-day life."—Kristina

Your Plan for the Project *(copy your plan on the Project Planner at the back of this book)*

Results *(mate's reaction, my reaction)*

Project 16

It's All About Her
Couch Time

*"The most precious possession that ever comes
To a man in this world
Is a woman's heart."*
JOSIAH G. HOLLAND

Your Project

She gets to pick the movie, TV show, or whatever she would like to do on the couch.

Guys, make sure you can dedicate a reasonable amount of time to this activity. No fair watching the clock or accidently changing the channel to *The Deadliest Catch* while she's getting the popcorn. (Hey, why is she getting the popcorn in the first place? This is a full-service evening.) Don't worry, your day is just around the corner.

Purpose of the Project

Couch time is a celebration of the best kind of love—comfortable love. See how author Paula Friedrichsen describes comfortable love in her book *The Man You Always Wanted Is the One You Already Have:*

> Comfortable love is like coming home after a hard day's work to the smell of beef stew simmering in the Crock-Pot. Comfortable love is like changing out of a business suit, nylons, and high heels into flannel jammies and fluffy

slippers. Comfortable love is like coming in from a raging winter storm to a cozy home warmed by a crackling fire.

In a day and age where the siren song of modern media promises women true and lasting happiness based on their income, material possessions, bust size, or hair color—marriage offers us *comfortable love.*

> Life is good when I can rest my head in my husband's lap and feel secure in the knowledge that I am loved.

Yesterday was Jeff's and my twenty-first wedding anniversary. We will go out to dinner next Saturday night to celebrate, and then snuggle on the couch to watch a movie together. And this is perfect. This is enough. This is my marriage.

You may be underwhelmed by our celebration plans. Maybe you're wondering, *Where's the trip to Paris?* or *Where's the diamond anniversary band?* (You know… like on the Zales commercial.) or *Won't there be a surprise getaway to a cozy bed and breakfast, where Jeff has arranged for chilled champagne and draws you a bubble bath?*

Uh…no. You see, that's just not Jeff's style. But he more than makes up for it. Because while unrealistic expectations and perfection in body and home are foisted upon women at every turn, my husband accepts me as I am. In a culture where an extreme makeover promises us fulfillment and happiness, my husband offers lasting love and enduring security.

Now don't get me wrong, if my mate surprised me with a trip to Paris, I would have my beret on before we hit the car door. Surprises are great, and wild romance is many a girl's dream. But life is good when I can rest my head in my husband's lap and feel secure in the knowledge that I am loved.

Prayer for Today

Dear God, I pray that not only do I grow in passion with my partner, but also in comfort.

Getting Creative

- Ask your wife earlier in the week what she would like your couch time to look like. Maybe it's watching a movie or just sitting and talking for a little while.
- If it's a movie, make sure you have it in your collection, ordered it from Netflix, or can pick it up at the library.
- Go the extra mile and have a favorite snack waiting. Chocolate usually works.

Project Reports

"I have to tell you I was not looking forward to this one. I thought for sure we would be watching some chick flick, but she put on a movie we had seen when we were dating. I got her Taco Bell nachos (her favorite), and we just relaxed. Great evening—for both of us."—Rod

Your Plan for the Project *(copy your plan on the Project Planner at the back of this book)*

Results *(mate's reaction, my reaction)*

Project 17

Removing Obstacles
Getting Rid of Something that Drives Your Spouse Crazy

"Marriage is not just spiritual communion,
it is also remembering to take out the trash."
JOYCE BROTHERS

Your Project

Take care of some little annoyance in your love's day.

Purpose of the Project

My friend Tina has an email signature that makes me stop and think every time I see it. It reads: "Be kinder than necessary, for everyone you meet is fighting some kind of battle" (Unknown).

Isn't that the truth? I try (I really do) to remember that sentiment when the person behind the counter rolls his eyes at my extravagant coffee order (hey, if I'm paying $4 for a cup of coffee, I don't think a grande nonfat misto with three pumps of sugar-free vanilla is out of line) or when there's a woman in front of me in the grocery store express line with 25 items on the conveyor belt below the sign that states "10 Items or Less." And she has coupons. And she is writing an out-of-state check. And she forgot her ID.

I try to remember that people are not placed on the planet to purposely annoy me.

I'm at my snarky best when I forget that life is hard for other people. I've been known to sigh loudly when I feel put upon by temperamental baristas or suburban housewives who can't count. Perhaps the coffee guy just broke up with his girlfriend or the woman in the supermarket has a sick father-in-law she's caring for at home and has only 20 minutes to do all of her shopping for the week.

Everyone is fighting some kind of battle.

When I remember this simple truth, acts of kindness toward seemingly undeserving people no longer appear so wildly out of place. When I remember this, I put the dollar I received in change in the tip jar on the coffee counter, or I let the harried woman with too many items get in front of me in line. It may be small, but this may be the only kindness they experience all day.

> It's good for me to remember that both action and words are currency that counts when it comes to filling up that love piggy bank.

Everyone is fighting some kind of battle. And that includes our spouse.

I need to remember to be exceedingly kind to my husband—whether he seems to be having a hard day or not. Whether I have judged he deserves it or not. As the apostle John reminds us, "Dear children, let's not merely say that we love each other; let us show the truth by our actions" (1 John 3:18 NLT).

Marriage—Where Taking Out the Garbage Means "I Love You"

"As you wish."

Guys love the humor, and girls swoon for the romance. Yep, it's the movie on everyone's top ten list—*The Princess Bride*.

A beautiful girl called Buttercup (played by Robin Wright-Penn) lives on a farm in the fictional country of Florin. She delights in verbally torturing the farmhand, Westley (Cary Elwes), by ordering him to perform nonsensical chores for her. Westley's only answer, every time, is, "As you wish," while really meaning, "I love you."

This perfectly illustrates where many of us get messed up in the whole love thing. Women are waiting to hear "I love you" while men are waiting to be recognized for the fact that they're saying "I love you" in the things they do.

Before I arrive home from a weekend trip, my husband does his best to rally the troops (three sometimes surly teenagers) and get the house in order. I usually come home to a sink empty of dishes and a diminished pile of dirty clothes on Mount Wash-Me.

My husband knows I love to hear the words "I love you," but I have also had to learn that he says it every day, in a variety of ways. He says it by:

- going to work each day
- taking out the trash (or making sure that one of our kids does)
- replacing the fluorescent lights in the laundry room
- replacing the empty toilet paper roll in the bathroom
- feeding the cat
- making the bed every single day of our married life (stand back, ladies, he's mine)

It's good for me to remember that both action and words are currency that counts when it comes to filling up that love piggy bank.

Guys, throw us a bone every once in a while. Work toward a heartfelt "I love you" at least once a day.

Girls, it's time to cut our guys some slack. Make sure you're recognizing all the ways your husband *shows* you he loves you, every day.

Prayer for Today

Dear God, help me to work outside my comfort zone to make sure my spouse knows every day that he or she is loved.

Getting Creative

- Fill up his gas tank.
- Replace the burned out lightbulbs in those hard-to-reach spots.
- Set the coffee pot the night before for his first cup in the morning.
- Restock all the bathrooms with toilet paper.
- Clear the fridge of all expired take-out containers.
- Match all of his solo socks.
- Change (or have changed) the oil in your mate's car.
- Call the repair guy you both have been procrastinating to call.
- Take an inventory of his toiletries and see what he is running low on; replace before he has to borrow your 12-year-old son's Axe deodorant.
- Mow the lawn.

Your Plan for the Project *(copy your plan on the Project Planner at the back of this book)*

Results *(mate's reaction, my reaction)*

Project 18

It's All About Him
Couch Time

*"The greatest gift you can give another
is the purity of your attention."*
RICHARD MOSS

Your Project

OK, ladies, now is not the time to pull out the BBC version of
Jane Austin's *Pride and Prejudice* (unless your husband is into
that kind of thing). This is a time to find a movie with lots of
action (and maybe even some gratuitous violence thrown in
for good measure). It's guy couch time at your house.

Purpose of the Project

Now it's his turn to pick the movie, TV show, or whatever he'd
like to do on the couch. Girls, this is a great excuse to snuggle up
with him and bury your face into his shoulder during the scary parts
of the movie.

Let me just put it out there. This is one of the harder projects for
me. It's not because I hate action movies (because for the most part,
I do) or because I hate snuggling on the couch (because I love it). It's
because I have to just *sit there*.

No laptop. No cell phone. No blog updates. No notepad to just
jot down a few things. Nothing. I just have to sit there and watch a
movie.

And that makes me a little bit nuts.

I always feel as though I should be doing something—anything—to get things done. I'm the person who listens to books on CD while driving to the store (instructional books, of course). I don't go for a walk without a ballpoint pen and an index card to make notes—while simultaneously listening to yet another instructional download on my iPod. I memorize Bible verses while cooking soup, and file papers while watching *Extreme Makeover: Home Edition*. (I figure if they can build a whole house, the least I can do is clear off my desk.) Danger isn't my middle name, but Multitasking is. Some would call it efficiency. My husband calls it a need for medication.

> It's a struggle to remember that any time I spend with my husband is never a waste of time.

So the thought of not getting anything done for 90 minutes is a little disconcerting. Especially when instead, I'm taking in a movie I have no interest in whatsoever. (I know, I know, "Selfish? Party of one?")

I do realize that while sitting there watching *Mythbusters* or *Storm Chasers* is not my idea of a good time, it is something my husband loves to share with me. Even if most of our time watching *Storm Chasers* includes me screaming at the TV, "Get indoors—can't you see that tornado? Who cares if you get great footage of that twister if you DIE IN THE PROCESS!"

And how can I complain when Roger can now name the past three winners of *Project Runway*? It's more than fair for me to have to sit there and watch boy TV.

It's a struggle to remember that any time I spend with my husband is never a waste of time. If I can just push the computer (or the book or the filing or the notepad) away for a moment, make sure the coffee table is laden with popcorn and Diet Cokes, and get snuggled on the couch with my husband and my favorite quilt, I know that not only am I going to have a good time, but my man will feel loved and honored.

Definitely worth putting down the Bic pens for the night.

Prayer for Today

Dear God, let me lay aside my own agenda for the moment and be what my spouse needs me to be.

Getting Creative

- You can watch something that is rented, downloaded, saved, or already in your movie collection. Just make sure it's something that the man of the family really wants to watch.

- For extra points, make sure appropriate snacks are available.

- This may be the evening to loosen up on the "no food in the living room" rule and enjoy a carpet picnic of Chinese food or takeout pizza. Lay down a blanket to create that picnic ambiance (and save the carpet from pesky spills).

Project Reports

"Um—who knew all the boy TV there was out there? It was so much fun just to sit next to my husband and hear him laugh. He has been so stressed out at work that it was great to see him relaxed and happy."—Marie

Your Plan for the Project *(copy your plan on the Project Planner at the back of this book)*

Results *(mate's reaction, my reaction)*

All the Kids Are Doing It
Text or Email Some Sweet Nothings

*"Words are, of course, the most powerful
drug used by mankind."*
RUDYARD KIPLING

Your Project

Text or email something fun or flirty to your love. No suggestions to "pick up milk on the way home" allowed.

Purpose of the Project

I want you to kick up the flirt-and-fun level just a notch today. Who knows, this may become such a fun part of your marriage that you develop carpal tunnel syndrome from flirting too much!

Remember when you were dating and you couldn't wait for your sweetie to call? Just hearing the phone ring made your heart skip a beat.

I bet that you've calmed down since then.

I know—it's hard to call her at work because you never know when you might be interrupting an important meeting. And it's hard to call him at work—he doesn't want to be whispering sweet nothings over the phone while the guys are listening.

> Remember when you were dating and you couldn't wait for your sweetie to call?

It's time to learn the art of "Text Flirt."

1. Figure out how to text on your cell phone.

2. If you can't figure it out, find any person under the age of 30 and hand her your cell phone. People born in the '80s and after have an extra compartment of their brain that those of us born before hip-hop are missing. Doesn't matter what kind of cell phone you have—they can figure out how to text.

3. Type something flirty and press send.

The beautiful thing is that you won't be interrupting your love at work—they can read that text (or email if that's the way you want to go) anytime they have a spare moment.

If you didn't grow up in the era of ROTFL (rolling on the floor laughing) and other text/instant message talk, here's a quick primer on some texting shortcuts you may find useful:

BBS: Be back soon

CM: Call me

CYE: Check your email

F2F: Face-to-face

HB: Hurry back

JFF: Just for fun

KOTC: Kiss on the cheek

SLAP: Sounds like a plan

TMB: Text me back

UGTBK: You've got to be kidding

DH: Dear husband

DW: Dear wife

Just a Warning

When I came up with this project, I thought it would be just a cute way to incorporate some flirting into your marriage. But over the past few months I have received several emails like the one below:

> "My husband was out of the country on business. I hadn't had the foresight to stick a card in his suitcase. So I used my camera phone to take a shirtless pic of myself, and I emailed it to his Blackberry. (And then immediately panicked that someone in his IT department would intercept!) No interception happened, and he was surprised, to say the least!"—Susan

I about fell off my chair when I read that.

Now, Roger will never receive a picture like that from me, but I think it's great that so many women are…let's just say, having a lot of fun with this project. If you can't be slightly scandalous with your spouse, then what is the fun of being married? (But please, please, please, only personal cell phones and email accounts—ones that neither your kids nor your boss have access to.)

Prayer for Today

Dear God, please let me be free in expressing my love for my mate. I pray they never have to guess about my love and admiration.

Project Report

> "I have to admit that I forgot about this project, so when my wife sent me a text, I was shocked because she had never texted anyone before in her life. Just the fact that she would go to the trouble to ask our daughter how to use the text feature on her phone made me appreciate her even more."—Brad

Your Plan for the Project *(copy your plan on the Project Planner at the back of this book)*

Results *(your mate's reaction, your reaction)*

Project 20

Clean Toilets Are Sexy
Help Out with One of Your Spouse's Chores

*"Many marriages would be better if the husband and the
wife clearly understood that they are on the same side."*
ZIG ZIGLAR

Your Project

Just for today take over one duty that you know your spouse
hates to do or is burned out doing.

Purpose of the Project

"Shotgun!"

As soon as I hear it I inwardly groan. The day both my kids were
old enough to safely ride in the front seat of the car, the fight began.
Who was going to ride up front?

We devised a number of elaborate systems to make sure that everything was fair. One kid would ride next to me on the way to school,
one on the way home. If it were an even numbered day, my daughter
would ride up front; on odd days, it would be my son's turn.

But no matter how diligently we kept track of turns, the kids were
never satisfied. It always seemed that the fairer things were, the more
cheated everyone felt.

This attitude isn't exclusive to our kids (and let me just put it out
there that my kids still do this, even though my son shaves and my
daughter is of dating age); it extends to adults as well.

So many times when I discuss the topic of this book, the person I'm speaking with says, "Yeah, I used to do those nice things for my spouse, but I never got anything in return." The sentiment is that if things aren't even, it's just not worth the effort.

A Spousal Bill of Rights

Recently I was reading a friend's blog when I noticed a link to "The Wife's Bill of Rights." I wondered what rights I had been missing out on and, more importantly, how I could start to claim some of them.

What was probably supposed to be an article with some funny musings ("We have the right to keep and bear tons of girly products") turned out to be mostly a list of "rights" that seemed just bitter and demanding, including statements such as, "We have the right to keep secrets" and "We have the right to healthy flirting."

> I thank God every day that He's not fair with me.

When either a husband or wife goes through marriage intent on protecting or enforcing his or her rights, little room is left for love and grace.

While 1 Corinthians 13 talks at length about what love *is*, it is also very clear about what love *is not*: "It does not dishonor others, it is not self-seeking, it is not easily angered, it keeps no record of wrongs" (1 Corinthians 13:5).

Several times my husband and I have had to rip up the mental scorecard tracking what our spouse "owed" us in our marriage. Things are never going to be fair. And they shouldn't be. Each of us should take Jesus' approach when we want things to be fair: "If anyone forces you to go one mile, go with them two miles" (Matthew 5:41).

I thank God every day that He's not fair with me. I have so much more than I deserve or even need. When I start to look at all the times when I feel as though I've been the extra-mile person in my marriage, I try to remember that fair is not something I should be striving for in any of my relationships.

In her article, "What Have You Done for Me Lately," posted on her website, speaker and writer Teresa Drake talks about recognizing the important contributions our spouses make by simply covering the basics:

> I used to associate the question, "What have you done for me lately?" with job performance, not marital partnership. During a stressful season in our marriage, however, I discovered that attitude lodged in my heart, provoking an explosion of anger toward my husband.
>
> In my mind I was a wonderful wife; the proverbial woman in the expression *behind every great man is a great woman*. In fact, one of my biggest claims to marital fame was that I packed/unpacked for Randy's business trips; something I started doing soon after we were married. I was so good, in fact, that I provided a clothing itinerary, detailing outfits for each event, down to the color of socks, shoes, ties and belts. At the time, Randy seemed more than grateful, even bragging to co-workers how I spoiled him with my deluxe packing.
>
> So when he stepped into the ring to spar over my *What Have You Done for Me Lately* challenge, I was surprised, but wasted no time delivering my one-two punch: that after 16 years I was still packing for him, despite my workload having increased exponentially.
>
> I hadn't anticipated this comeback: "Uh-huh, that's just what you normally do now. It's not something special anymore."
>
> I had no fitting reply. I stormed out of the room further convinced I was taken for granted. That Randy might feel the same way never crossed my mind.
>
> After all, the only thing he does all day is work. That's nothing compared to my accomplishments on any given day, I thought. On weekends he makes pancakes for breakfast, pays the bills, and usually cooks dinner, too. There's nothing extraordinary about that. It's just what he...normally does.

Oh.

That was my light-bulb moment. I realized that taking some-one for granted had insidiously become a two-way street, right through the middle of our home.

"For by the grace given to me I say to everyone among you not to think of yourself more highly than you ought to think, but to think with sober judgment, each according to the measure of faith that God has assigned" (Romans 12:3).

I now understand that Randy does what he normally does because that's how he demonstrates his love and commitment to me and our family, that he delights in lightening my load and, occasionally, surprising me, just because.

I'm learning to recognize blessings that are both big and small; and in doing so, I've discovered a heartwarming answer those few times I've found myself pondering...what have you done for me lately?

Prayer for Today

Dear God, may I experience Your joy today as I serve my mate by helping to lighten his (or her) load.

Getting Creative

- It doesn't matter how it gets done. Some of the most roman-tic words my husband whispers to me are, "Would you like me to pick up something for dinner?"

- When your spouse does a chore for you, no fair criticizing her if it's not done to your standards. If you constantly cri-tique other people's work, that might be why your spouse isn't willing to jump in and help sometimes. Just something to think about.

Project Reports

"I am absolutely amazed at how much my attitude has changed! I am looking at my husband differently, and I'm finding myself trying to find more than one thing to do for him per day. Some things are small and probably won't be noticed, but that doesn't really matter to me in the long run."—Wendy

Your Plan for the Project *(copy your plan on the Project Planner at the back of this book)*

Results *(mate's reaction, your reaction)*

Project 21

What I Like About You

You Really Know How to Dance, How to Pay the Bills, How to Be Nice to My Mom

"Nothing is more honorable than a grateful heart."

SENECA

Your Project

> In the space provided on page 205, write down ten things you like about your mate. Then tonight before you go to sleep, read the list to your spouse.

In an earlier chapter, I had you write down why you were in love with that person sitting across the table from you. Now I want you to write down the things you *like* about him or her. While you may not have fallen in love with your wife because she makes a mean chicken cacciatore, that could fall into the "like" category. Think of some of the fun and silly stuff that makes life together great.

Purpose of the Project

All too often we're quick to grumble and complain, detailing the nitty-gritty things in our marriage or spouse that drive us nuts. Most couples are well aware of the things their spouse thinks they do wrong or could do better.

Today you can make sure your spouse knows all the wonderful

things you adore about her (or him); the things she says, does, believes—whatever you like about your mate. Remember, "the tongue has the power of life and death" (Proverbs 18:21).

"Fred Rogers, will you be proud of me?"

I read these words in Tim Madigan's excellent book, *I'm Proud of You*, in which he tells his personal story as a newspaper journalist whose life was falling apart. He and his wife were on the ragged edge of divorce, his drinking had gotten out of control, and in every way—mentally, spiritually, physically, and emotionally—he was on the brink. After being sent on assignment to interview the famous Mr. Rogers, Madigan and the TV legend formed a profound friendship unlike any he'd ever experienced before. Mr. Rogers provided much of what seemed to be missing from Madigan's life—someone to encourage him, someone to be proud of him.

> We often have no idea the power that our words carry.

We often have no idea the power that our words carry in our circle of influence. The power to encourage or discourage, the power to shape how other people see themselves.

If someone were to ask your spouse, "Why is your husband (or wife) proud of you?" would she have an answer?

Make sure your spouse knows what you admire about him or her. You may be the only person who offers such encouragement today.

Prayer for Today

Dear God, thank You for my spouse. You have given me just the right person to grow me to become more like You.

Getting Creative

Below is a quick list of statements you could say to your spouse:

- You make the bed every day, making coming home so much nicer.
- You work long hours to support our family, helping me feel more secure.
- You always make sure we have my kind of milk in the house.
- You are nice to my friends and always make them feel welcome.
- You never complain when I say, "Can we just order in tonight?"
- You never erase my shows on TiVo.
- You watch guy/girl movies with me.
- You're a great dad (or mom).

Now it's your turn:

1.
2.
3.
4.
5.
6.
7.
8.
9.
10.

Project Reports

"One of my favorite projects was 'What I Like About You.' It was very easy to come up with ten things I like about Karyn.

I think the interesting thing about this particular day was to express things that you'd assume your mate would know you think about them. I really enjoyed hearing Karyn read her list to me."—Rob

"The things I heard in this activity were shocking. He likes my 'athletic build'? At first I thought this was a joke, but the reality was that he enjoys that we can play golf together and that I can hold my own on the course and have a great time doing it. It was interesting to hear his perspective of the fad of skinny girls and that he loves me just the way I am!"—Kristina

"We enjoyed doing 'What I Like About You.' I could have written forever about the qualities of my wife and how much I love her. I was totally amazed about the similarities we have in common with each other. After 20 years of marriage you come to recognize you are one flesh, not only physically but mentally as well."—Harlenn

Your Plan for the Project *(copy your plan on the Project Planner at the back of this book)*

Results *(mate's reaction, my reaction)*

Major Project 3

Date Your Mate
Double Your Pleasure, Double Your Fun

Your Project

Go out with another couple. Have the men plan together the details for the date—a date you ladies will love.

Purpose of the Project

Instead of going through all the reasons why I want the guys to team up and plan your date, I'm going to show you what one set of couples planned for their double date. I hope you will be as inspired as I was.

Chris and Lee (my friend Kristina's husband) took the double date project very seriously. They banded together like all men do and sent each other emails for a couple of days planning the strategy. Chris would be in charge of the invitations, and Lee would be in charge of the reservations.

A couple of weeks before the date, Kristina and I received our invitations (which really looked like wedding invitations). Mine was waiting for me on the couch when I was about to settle in for the night. It was really cute the way Chris snuggled up to me while I opened it. He just loves to see my face when I'm surprised.

The invitation was beautifully written and truly brought a

tear to my eye. It was the thought and intention behind it that was so touching.

The invitation was for a romantic dinner at Forbes Mill Steakhouse, followed by a night of Bunco fun with our couples' Bunco group. (Bunco was already on the calendar, so they piggy-backed onto that…such a manly, efficient thing to do!)

When we got to the restaurant on the night of the big date, we found an intimate table for four. There waiting for us was a personalized menu and two vases filled with our favorite flowers (gerber daisy for me; orchid for Kristina). Lee had gone to the florist ahead of time and took the flowers to the restaurant. After a fabulous dinner, we headed over to Bunco and continued the fun.

> "Using their creativity and working together to make us happy made them happy."

We (the girls) usually do everything: think of the date, plan the date, arrange for the sitter, etc. Not that they're complaining, but the guys don't even get a *chance* to plan anything. If it hadn't been for this project, I don't think we would have *given* them the opportunity to plan…and plan they did!

What impressed me the most was that they:

1. talked about the evening ahead of time
2. had "to-dos"—which they accomplished, and
3. paid attention to detail (which, let's face it, men sometimes have a hard time doing)

When we talked about it later, Chris said he and Lee had such a great time doing this for us. Using their creativity and working together to make us happy made them happy. After hearing this, my heart *melted*!

—Camilla

Prayer for Today

Dear God, fill us with Your creativity as we plan our double date. May our evening together be a special time we will look back on with many happy memories.

Getting Creative

- Meet at Starbucks for a cup of coffee.
- Have another couple over for a barbecue and s'mores.
- Go go-cart racing together.
- Go miniature golfing on a warm night.
- Do lunch after church.
- Work on a service project together.

Your Plan for the Project *(copy your plan on the Project Planner at the back of this book)*

Results *(your mate's reaction, your reaction)*

Sex
Ladies, It's Ladies' Night

"Sex hasn't been the same since women started enjoying it."
Lewis Grizzard

Your Bonus Project

If I'm expecting the guys to plan a date for this week, it's only fair that the girls do a little planning of their own. Ladies, I want you to be the ones who get things rolling in this area this week. You suggest the time (or maybe keep it a surprise if your husband enjoys that kind of thing), set the mood, and when it comes to lingerie, if your guy is a fan, it's your time to "suit up"!

Guys, make sure to keep this week extra flirty and helpful. Trust me, the more dishes that are done during the week, the more relaxed and romantic your wife is going to be when it's time for your very special date.

Prayer for Today

God, thank You for Your gift of sex in our marriage. Help me to enjoy my mate as fully as You have intended.

Your Plan for the Project *(copy your plan on the Project Planner at the back of this book)*

Results *(mate's reaction, my reaction)*

Tools of
Happy Habits for
Every Couple

Project Planner

Consider this the place to put the CliffsNotes of your marriage project. Project managers have told me over and over that it was great to have their entire plan laid out on just a couple of pieces of paper so they could make copies and refer to it often.

- Write down one or two sentences about what your plan is for each day.

- Make copies of this plan to share with your accountability partners to help keep you on track.

- Make some extra copies for yourself. Leave one at the office, one in your purse or daily planner, and one in your Bible. That way, no matter where you are, you'll know what your project is for today and be able to plan for what's coming up.

- As you complete the projects, make sure you give yourself a checkmark on your planner. Nothing feels quite as satisfying on a busy day as a "project accomplished" checkmark.

You can download a copy here: http://www.kathilipp.com/happy habits/downloads/projectplanner

Week One

Sunday: Project 1   ☐ check when completed
Your plan for the project:

Monday: Project 2   ☐ check when completed
Your plan for the project:

Tuesday: Project 3   ☐ check when completed
Your plan for the project:

Wednesday: Project 4   ☐ check when completed
Your plan for the project:

Thursday: Project 5   ☐ check when completed
Your plan for the project:

Friday: Project 6   ☐ check when completed
Your plan for the project:

Saturday: Project 7   ☐ check when completed
Your plan for the project:

Major Project 1   ☐ check when completed
Your plan for the project:

Bonus Project 1   ☐ check when completed
Your plan for the project:

Week Two

Sunday: Project 8   ☐ check when completed
Your plan for the project:

Monday: Project 9   ☐ check when completed
Your plan for the project:

Tuesday: Project 10   ☐ check when completed
Your plan for the project:

Wednesday: Project 11   ☐ check when completed
Your plan for the project:

Thursday: Project 12   ☐ check when completed
Your plan for the project:

Friday: Project 13   ☐ check when completed
Your plan for the project:

Saturday: Project 14   ☐ check when completed
Your plan for the project:

Major Project 2   ☐ check when completed
Your plan for the project:

Bonus Project 2   ☐ check when completed
Your plan for the project:

Week Three

Sunday: Project 15   ☐ check when completed
Your plan for the project:

Monday: Project 16   ☐ check when completed
Your plan for the project:

Tuesday: Project 17   ☐ check when completed
Your plan for the project:

Wednesday: Project 18   ☐ check when completed
Your plan for the project:

Thursday: Project 19   ☐ check when completed
Your plan for the project:

Friday: Project 20   ☐ check when completed
Your plan for the project:

Saturday: Project 21   ☐ check when completed
Your plan for the project:

Major Project 3   ☐ check when completed
Your plan for the project:

Bonus Project 3   ☐ check when completed
Your plan for the project:

Recommended Resources

For Men Only: A Straightforward Guide to the Inner Lives of Women by Shaunti Feldhahn and Jeff Feldhahn

For Women Only: A Straightforward Guide to the Inner Lives of Men by Shaunti Feldhahn

Getting the Love You Want: A Guide for Couples by Harville Hendrix

How to Save Your Marriage Alone by Ed Wheat

Avoiding the Greener Grass Syndrome: How to Grow Affair Proof Hedges Around Your Marriage by Nancy C. Anderson

I'm Proud of You: Life Lessons from My Friend Fred Rogers by Tim Madigan

Laugh Your Way to a Better Marriage: Unlocking the Secrets to Life, Love, and Marriage by Mark Gungor

The Man You Always Wanted Is the One You Already Have by Paula Friedrichsen

Red-Hot Monogamy: Making Your Marriage Sizzle by Bill Farrel and Pam Farrel

Sex Begins in the Kitchen: Creating Intimacy to Make Your Marriage Sizzle by Kevin Leman

Sheet Music: Uncovering the Secrets of Sexual Intimacy in Marriage by Kevin Leman

When Two Become One: Enhancing Sexual Intimacy in Marriage by Christopher and Rachel McCluskey

Dear Reader,

Thanks for being a part of *Happy Habits for Every Couple*. One of the greatest privileges I have is to hear back from the people who have used my books. I would love to stay in touch.

WEBSITE: www.KathiLipp.com
FACEBOOK: facebook.com/authorkathilipp
TWITTER: twitter.com/kathilipp

MAIL: Kathi Lipp
171 Branham Lane
Suite 10-122
San Jose, CA 95136

In His Grace,

Kathi Lipp

Also by Kathi Lipp:

The Husband Project
21 Days of Loving Your Man—on Purpose and with a Plan

Keeping a marriage healthy is all about the details—the daily actions and interactions in which husbands and wives lift each other up and offer support, encouragement, and love. In *The Husband Project* women will discover fun and creative ways to bring back that lovin' feeling and remind their husbands—and themselves—why they married in the first place.

Using the sense of humor that draws thousands of women a year to hear her speak, Kathi Lipp shows wives through simple daily action plans how they can bring the fun back into their relationship even amidst their busy schedules.

The Husband Project is an indispensable resource for the wife who desires to

- discover the unique plan God has for her marriage and her role as a wife
- create a plan to love her husband "on purpose"
- support and encourage other wives who want to make their marriage a priority
- experience release from the guilt of "not being enough"

The Husband Project is for every woman who desires to bring more joy into her marriage but just needs a little help setting a plan into action.

The Get Yourself Organized Project

21 Steps to Less Mess and Stress

Finally, an organizational book for women who have given up trying to be Martha Stewart but still desire some semblance of order in their lives.

Most organizational books are written by and for people who are naturally structured and orderly. For the woman who is more ADD than type A, the advice sounds terrific but seldom works. These women are looking for help that takes into account their free-spirited outlook while providing tips and tricks they can easily follow to live a more organized life.

Kathi Lipp, author of *The Husband Project* and other "project" books, is just the author to address this need. In her inimitable style, she offers

- easy and effective ways you can restore peace to your everyday life
- simple and manageable long-term solutions for organizing any room in your home (and keeping it that way)
- a realistic way to de-stress a busy schedule
- strategies for efficient shopping, meal preparation, cleaning, and more

Full of helpful tips and abundant good humor, *The Get Yourself Organized Project* will enable you to spend your time living and enjoying life rather than organizing your sock drawer.

21 Ways to Connect with Your Kids

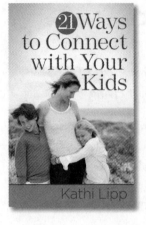

Parents spend a good chunk of time making sure their kids are okay—they're getting good grades, doing their chores, and just enough cleaning that their rooms won't be condemned if the Board of Health happens to drop by. *21 Ways to Connect with Your Kids* offers a straightforward, workable plan that coaches you to do one simple thing each day for three weeks to connect with your kids.

Daily connection ideas include:

- planning a family fun night
- telling your child what you like about them
- developing a character growth chart
- writing a love note to your child
- working together on a family project

Written in Kathi's warm and personable but thought-provoking tone, this book will motivate you to incorporate great relationship habits into your daily life and give you confidence that you can connect with your kids even in the midst of busy schedules.

The Cure for the "Perfect" Life

12 Ways to Stop Trying Harder and Start Living Braver

Are you crumbling under the burden of perfection? You know the expectations are unreasonable—even unreachable. And when everyone else seems more together than you, where do you turn for help?

Meet Kathi, a disguised perfectionist always looking to put everyone else's needs above her own, and Cheri, a formerly confused and exhausted poster girl for playing it safe. They've struggled just like you—and found the cure. With unabashed empathy and humor, they invite you to take part in their rebellion against perfection. Step-by-step they'll teach you how to challenge and change unhealthy beliefs. As they free you from always seeking more or needing approval of others, you'll discover a new, braver way of living. At last, you'll exchange outdated views of who you *should be* for a clearer vision of *who you are* in Christ.

The truth is you don't have to be perfect. You just have to be brave enough to read this book.